*M*anagement Accounting for Financial Institutions

The Complete Desktop
Reference Guide ————————————

Revised Edition

Leonard P. Cole

A BankLine Publication

PROBUS
PUBLISHING

Chicago, Illinois
Cambridge, England

BANK**LINE**™
A BankLine Publication

ISBN 1-55738-738-9

Printed in the United States of America

BB

1 2 3 4 5 6 7 8 9 0

CB

I would like to give special thanks and recognition
to my wife Lynn
who devoted many hours of her time
toward the completion of this book.

Table of Contents

PART III: ISSUES

List of Figures

List of Figures

Preface

Today's financial institution management needs reliable and consistent information for making decisions. Information on costs, profitability, planning, and risk is necessary to manage a financial institution. For example, information on risk is vital in coping with today's volatile business environment.

A financial institution's management must know the cost of doing business and how to price products. These are among the many things a financial institution manager must comprehend. This support information has to be available to make decisions. Costs must be known by category, e.g., salaries, organization, and product. In many cases, it also is helpful to know costs by major customers.

Information on profitability is essential, as it is derived by organization, product, and major customer. Management thereby can decide which business segments to continue, change, or cancel.

Information must be timely, clear, and concise to formulate tactical and strategic planning for a financial institution. A well-executed tactical plan will complement a strategic plan, which requires time to prepare.

Interest rate volatility is here to stay. The days of stable interest rates may never return. This is just one risk among at least seven risk categories a financial institution faces. More on risks will be discussed later.

A well-managed financial institution requires good people and a focus on information needed to make wise decisions. This book has been written with these thoughts in mind and provides an overview of the subjects mentioned. It also is a quick reference guide.

Management accounting provides decision information to executives. Management accounting reports performance, risk, and other factors bearing on the status of an organization and interprets and gives meaning to these factors. Management accounting contrasts to financial accounting. The latter's aim is to report the institution's condition and performance from a financial standpoint. Financial accounting is not concerned with behavioral factors such as cooperation between departments within an institution, only finances.

This book has three major parts with 10 chapters that address planning, management control, and issues.

Part I—Planning

Chapter 1 describes how management accounting affects high performance in financial institutions. The characteristics of a well-managed institution are covered, with emphasis on the dissemination of information and how to use it. Management style and other behavioral dimensions affecting performance reporting also are discussed. A profile of the inner workings of a high-performance financial institution is a part of this chapter. The question, "What must we do to optimize our performance?" is answered. The critical role of executive information and how it helps an institution achieve top performance is the basis for discussion in this book.

Chapter 2 details strategic planning in a basic step-by-step process. The benefits of planning annually also are discussed.

Chapter 3 covers tactical planning and capital budgeting. An overview of the planning process for revenue, expenses, and business activity is presented. How to design, develop, and implement a tactical planning system is explained. How to integrate an institution's strategic plan with its tactical (opening) plan is covered. This chapter also provides an overview of the planning process in addition to exploring what management must think about and do.

Part II—Management Control

The bigger picture—management information reporting systems—is covered in Chapter 4, describing how to design, develop, implement, and use functional reporting systems. This includes reporting on profitability, activity, and performance for organization, product, and customer dimensions. An integrated reporting functional design also is discussed.

Cost and profitability reporting are covered in Chapter 5. The material is condensed and provides a brief overview of financial institution costing. The emphasis, however, is on designing a cost and profitability reporting system to serve your institution. The text includes suggestions on how to avoid pitfalls and costly mistakes. Checklists are provided for evaluating your current system and determining your needs. What to do with identified systems gaps also is explored.

Asset and liability management (ALM) is a complex subject. A person who wants a brief overview of the subject and how the process works will find Chapter 6 useful. It covers areas within ALM that one should consider in setting up a basic ALM function.

Chapter 6 is a good place to start for understanding the basics of the subject. It covers maturity and interest rate gap management, simulation, duration, pricing, liquidity, contingency funding planning, float analysis, and cost of capital. Many other subjects are included.

Chapter 7 provides ideas and report formats for measuring performance and risk. Operating performance frequently is complex to administer on a comprehensive basis. However, ways to focus on key items will alert you to what is happening. The same goes for risk measurement. Interest rate risk, credit risk, liquidity risk, foreign exchange risk, transfer risk, sector risk, and operating risk all concern financial institutions today. This chapter has suggestions on how to cope with each risk.

Part III—Issues

Chapter 8 deals with funds transfer pricing (funds valuation), an important issue being debated and addressed in many financial institutions today.

Chapter 9 covers allocation issues, such as equity allocation and loan loss allocation.

Chapter 10 is devoted to recovery and reporting issues, including overhead recovery reporting and shadow accounting.

The alternatives and implications within each issue are explained. There is not necessarily a single correct method or approach for resolving each of the issues. Resolution comes easier when an institution knows the behavior it wants as a result of a particular methodology. An example of this is using a single-pool rate in funds transfer pricing as opposed to multiple pools. This method may work better in one institution than another, attributable to several factors in an individual institution's information systems. All of this will be discussed in this book.

The function of management accounting is to provide information for executive decision making. It should provide a focus on the relevant factors affecting performance and risk. The practitioner is called on to research, sort, and identify issues that influence these factors. Keen judgment is needed to determine what is important and relevant.

This book is written for two audiences: (1) financial institution executives and directors who are accountable for the performance of an institution and have little time to delve extensively into pertinent issues and subjects but yet need to respond intelligently to them; and (2) CFOs, controllers, and management accountants who need additional insight on these subjects. It arms the executive with basic knowledge on relevant management issues. Some thoughts for the executive on what questions to ask to guarantee that the institution is operating properly are also provided.

This book serves as a reference for individuals who have busy and demanding schedules but need to know.

Part I

Planning

1

Management Accounting and High-Performance Financial Institutions

I f you were to begin a list of what constitutes a high-performance financial institution you probably would come up with ideas that fall into several subject areas. First on your list probably would be something about a good management team, the core of a top-performing institution. All else is what this team does.

At the top of the list of what they do probably would be something on good information flow, because a well-managed institution has a good information structure. This book provides tools for the executive to build a strong information reporting structure in his or her institution.

A high-performance financial institution is characterized by:

- A well-organized and active management team that anticipates what must be done and takes the initiative to do it. The team must communicate freely, collaborate to accomplish the institution's purposes, initiate new thinking, make things happen, know what is occurring, and monitor performance closely.

- A clear strategy and mission: Everyone in the organization has a sense of purpose and direction, with goals and strategy clearly laid out.

- A highly tuned organization that is precise, efficient, and effective, where each employee is accountable for his or her performance. The expected results of meetings are stated before they occur. Project goals are defined, and projected results are monitored closely to add value.

- A well-organized set of management information reports that go to the management team. The reports give management needed information. They also respond to management's style and are easy to read, concise, and timely.

- A clarity of image, management style, expectations, goals, communications, and controls. The organization thrives on precision and each person knows his or her job and is used to the fullest extent of ability and skill.

This chapter sets the stage for understanding the importance of management accounting's role within an institution. Management depends on concise and relevant information to carry on daily duties. When properly deployed, management accounting is a tool for achieving high performance in a financial institution. The tool provides measurements of performance, warnings on risk, information for decisions, and data for planning.

We will discuss here what an institution has to do with information to achieve optimum performance. Once the performance criteria are described, then management accounting's role can be outlined. Management accountants should be consulted on what they view as criteria for top performance. Their advice is valuable in determining what is relevant.

Being a High-Performance Financial Institution

If asked about ROA and ROE objectives, most managers would think an ROA of 1.50 percent and an ROE of 20 percent would be difficult to achieve, especially for large institutions. However, most would agree these goals are highly desirable.

But what energizes a highly profitable institution with a premier image? To begin with, it has strong leadership but with a style that doesn't have to be authoritarian. A leader motivates people rather than dominates them—someone who has vision and sense of direction, and can articulate goals. This leadership inspires and influences others to fulfill stated goals. A leader works effectively and productively with others and communicates easily.

An institution where everyone has a sense of direction and key purpose is one where the message of the leadership's mission has reached all levels of the organization. A good leader exudes confidence to his or her organization.

It is important that each employee be held accountable for his or her effectiveness in achieving goals. Effectiveness is doing what has to be done with optimum efficiency. Efficiency is the ability to produce a desired effect with a minimum of effort. If management has created a tightly woven organization, each person will know how well he or she is contributing to stated goals. The key to getting things done is worker accountability.

Each employee should be conscious of time and the value of his or her contributions to the institution. This is especially true when it comes to meetings in institutions that have a lot of committees and project groups. A well-run institution will have people managing committees and projects. These managers will get others to show up on time, have a clearly stated agenda, and get results as quickly as possible. Managers who know how to communicate clearly can keep a meeting on track. Before each meeting, they should state the expected results of the meeting.

During the meetings, the managers keep people focused on the purposes and objectives. At the end of each meeting they should reiterate decisions, actions items, and completion dates. The managers usually get commitments on who is to do what and when. If another meeting is necessary the date, time, and location should be decided. The idea here is that nothing should be casual in the pace, content, purpose, and resolution of meetings. The managers need to keep the fire going. Their job is to instill energy and nothing should be left to chance. An organization should be well-organized and action oriented.

An institution high in energy conveys a positive message that enhances its image. This is true when people see that things happen at your institution. Quick responses to customers, clear routing of inquiries, and fast processing send messages that your institution is sharp and efficient. The image your institution conveys is important because it tells customers, community, investors, and employees how organized your institution is. That will project the image to the audience. Institutions with a good public image know how to respond, have good communications, and project a clear message. In today's deregulated environment, given similarities of products and services, image can be a deciding success factor.

How well an institution uses its resources definitely affects performance. The institution has two important resources: people and money. How the two are deployed makes the difference in a financial institution's performance.

To use staff resources optimally requires the following:

- Using part-time staff at peak hours.
- Keeping staff support functions to a minimum.
- Having a salary structure that attracts high-caliber, hard-working people.
- Having an incentive program to motivate the staff.
- Having a staff and compensation growth tracking program that dissuades managers from adding unnecessary staff.
- Tracking all projects that use continuous staff and financial resources, and holding managers accountable for project completions, cost control, and realization of stated benefits.
- Having a work program where no one is idle; during slack periods, the staff is assigned to alternative tasks.

A financial institution managing its financial resources to the optimum does the following:

- Has an active asset/liability management committee.
- Has a strategy and policy for optimizing its interest spread—both on asset pricing and funds acquisitions.
- Keeps noninterest expenses to a minimum and holds managers accountable.
- Is active in tactical (operating) and strategic planning.
- Has a consistent pricing strategy for noncredit products.

A well-managed institution also has a good management accounting program. It tells management how its resources are being managed. Such information serves management's needs at all levels. A good management accounting program does the following:

- Tells the cost and profitability of doing business by organization, product, and major customer.
- Avoids surprises.
- Allows all managers to explain their performance as it is reported.
- Lets everyone participate in planning, and plan-to-actual reporting is used as a management tool.
- Provides timely, accurate, relevant, and understandable reporting.
- Ensures that only one set of numbers is floating around the institution.
- Reduces or eliminates complaints about information availability.

Deciding What Information Is Necessary

Because financial institutions are people intensive, the inclination is to disseminate much information: some essential, some nice to know, and some unnecessary. Some institutions devote a great deal of time and effort reducing their information flow, eliminating unnecessary reports and trimming distribution lists.

It takes time to prepare reports, distribute them, and read them. Information crucial to running an organization should be given top priority. If each manager were to check his or her "out box" and "in box" and ask, "Is this really necessary?" and react accordingly, you probably would see a decline in paper passing from one box to another.

Managers should be kept informed but within practical limits. All memoranda and reports should have value-added qualities. In a well-managed organization, managers keep information concise and on a need-to-know basis. They discourage reports fraught with "nice-to-know" but unnecessary information. Their information has sufficient analysis and formats are clear and to the point. There is no guessing on what the information means. Also, the management culture is such that no manager feels the need to be on every distribution list. Too, no manager should feel he or she must manufacture reports and memoranda to get attention. Only relevant and necessary information is produced and distributed to the institution's officers.

Profiles in Profitability

Managing profitability is an everyday task. It begins with optimal use of human and financial resources to maximize your marketplace opportunities. A financial institution can use its resources to achieve the highest profitability possible by closely managing the following areas:

- Credit Product Pricing—Set prices at levels that recover potential credit and interest-rate risk. Establish target spreads and monitor results closely.

- Float Management—Identify, reduce, or charge for unfavorable float.

- Asset Growth—Keep a comfortable growth pace. Avoid concentration on a specific industry or region. Maintain a stringent credit quality policy. Keep capital constraints in mind.

- Liability Growth—Keep purchased funds at a comfortable and safe level. Signal a halt to asset growth when purchased funds reach a defined maximum threshold.

- Noncredit Services—Develop a consistent pricing policy. Set prices above costs. Charge the highest price possible.

- Noninterest Expenses—Monitor staff costs and growth closely. Hold departments accountable for budget compliance. Review major expense categories in the budget and question the value or worth of planned expenses.

- Capital Expenditures—Review whether expenditures will bring a required return or meet management's needs.

A commitment to following up on consistent and timely pricing while tracking and correcting budget variances helps an institution toward maximum profitability.

Focusing on Pressure Points

The top officers of a well-managed organization know where their institution is vulnerable. They also have timely information that keeps them posted on vulnerable areas. This provides a necessary comfort factor. The information also helps the executives adjust points of pressure when necessary. No executive wants to watch helplessly while an out-of-control situation erodes the institution's resources. This is why some institutions have safeguards that report exceptions so executives can focus on pressure points and make timely adjustments when needed.

These safeguards are control levers, tools to make adjustments. They are preventive and corrective actions, usually predetermined by policy. In establishing controls, management thinks through the possible risks the institution could face and establishes policy to minimize the risk. Management also prescribes what action should be taken if the occasion arises. An example is data-processing disaster recovery: To begin with, DP management has policies and procedures to minimize controllable risk. But a plan also is needed for coping with the unforeseen adversity. The plan should have procedures to bring DP back into operation. Top financial institution officers need to know about the plan so they would have steady control over operational recovery. Another example is processing critical information. If a backlog occurs, the institution could be vulnerable and management must know when a condition like this occurs to be able to correct it.

A good information reporting structure is needed for alerting management to impending difficulties so it can take preventive action.

Risks in Financial Institutions

There are at least seven types of risk in financial institutions. They include credit risk, interest-rate risk, liquidity risk, foreign exchange risk, geographic risk, operating risk, and industry risk. Each one can significantly impair or improve profitability. Top management should enjoy a comfort factor in knowing these risks are being managed properly. No chief executive officer (CEO) wants to be left wondering if any problems exist that he or she is unaware of.

Here's a brief look at each risk factor. Credit risk has to do with loan quality, involving the risk of a borrower not repaying a loan. All financial institutions want good-quality performing loans. By measuring and managing loan diversification risk can be minimized. For example, money should not be lent to only one customer or one industry.

Obviously, the important factor in this risk is to lend to those who will pay back loans. Therefore, a loan application must be screened and reviewed stringently. Once on the books, a loan must be monitored closely. Account officers have to keep abreast of late payments and other exceptions and be alert to what is gong on in the customer's business, and top management needs to know the degree of this risk.

Comfort in interest-rate risk is having a positive spread between assets and liabilities. However, there is the possibility that net interest income and/or the value of assets can be impaired by interest rate movements. This risk may be minimized by active asset and liability management.

Liquidity risk is the inability to fund assets or meet withdrawal demands. This risk can be minimized by being able to liquidate assets or increase liabilities over a short term to satisfy money requirements. Managing assets and maturities of liabilities is important here. Liquidity risk also is minimized by a healthy mix of core deposits.

Foreign exchange risk is the chance of one's currency or a position in another currency losing value, with a decline harming earnings.

Geographic risk deals with economic, political, and currency-transfer policy of a country or region. It is the risk that events in a geographic area can injure business and thereby impair financial institutions because they are unable to collect on loans. Transfer risk involves having profits being restricted to the country where they were earned.

Operating risk relates to all factors attributable to an institution's function such as fraud or a snafu, the risk of something not getting done.

Industry risk deals with the volatility of an economic segment such as oil, gas, or agriculture.

These risks need to be tracked and reported to management.

Performance Measurement

An institution can measure performance in several ways. Widely used measurements include financial, operating, and marketing performance.

Financial information can be broken down into the following categories: profitability; earnings; capital adequacy; credit risk management; and asset/liability management. Operating performance can be measured by staffing levels and overhead ratios. Marketing effectiveness covers such target objectives as new loans, new deposits, and share of market.

All of these should be measured against a plan. These data also can be graphed to show a trend pictorially. Well-managed institutions have performance measurement reports that are concise, clear, and easy to understand. Some organizations appropriately call them "management control reports." They provide management with necessary control levers. Management can read them, make informed decisions, and take action. The main thrust of performance reporting is to flag areas needing attention and pin down accountability.

A detailed explanation and sample report package is in Chapter 7.

Developing Strategies

When rapid change occurs in the marketplace, financial institutions must react quickly to remain current. Tactical responses to product changes by a competitor don't always have to happen. Sometimes seeing what happens and reacting later makes good sense. An institution that has a deliberate and determined course of direction is not disoriented when the competition makes a surprise move. An institution should be so well-organized it can assess changes, decide what to do, and then carry out a predetermined plan. All tactical short-term responses should be compatible with the financial institution's strategic or long-term plan.

Strategy development begins with a vision on where your institution wants to be at some future date. This vision incorporates organization structure, staff quality, products, marketplace, image, and location. Then the vision must be translated into a plan on how to get there, listing specific actions. Having a strategic plan helps prevent illogical or unreasoned reactions to a competitor's moves and instills stability and consistency.

Active Bank Management

Managers make things happen, usually through the actions of others. An active management team will have the kind of managers who are thinkers that seize opportunities. They anticipate needs and prepare for them. They are action oriented but never overreact. Such forward-thinking managers instill vitality in an organization.

This kind of managing begins with the CEO who sets the tone. Once the CEO's pressure for ideas and plans is felt, lower managers will react according to their value system of higher goals.

The future challenges of financial institutions require an active stance so financial institutions can maintain their business of providing financial services and earning acceptable returns for stockholders. The functions of management accounting and management-information reporting help financial institutions achieve those goals.

Management Accounting Supports High-Performance Financial Institution Management

The CEO who has a good information-reporting structure has a better chance of guiding the institution toward high performance than one who doesn't. Good information arises from a good management-accounting program—an important tool for providing decision-making information.

In a high-performance financial institution, you will find that managers use information effectively. Let's take an example of a high-performance institution. Call it First Performance Financial Institution. When you walk into its CEO's office, his desk is clear except for a chairman's reporting package, which is a summary of the institution's performance for last month. It arrived a week after the month ended.

The CEO can read it in an hour and have a good idea of what happened last month. He keeps it on his desk as a handy reference but more importantly as a management tool.

The chief's desk is clear because reports to him are unified, highly focused, and only sent on a need-to-know basis. Exceptions to normal performance are flagged for his attention. Junk mail is culled by the CEO's secretary.

The "chairman's package" tells him, allotting a page for each item, the following data:

- Where the institution made money last month (operating profitability).
- How the institution is performing by comparison with its goals (both operational and strategic).
- What contributed to profit changes from the preceding month.
- What the balance sheet trend indicates.
- Exceptions in performance flagged by risk categories, with recommended actions (early warnings).

- How the institution performed with its peer group the preceding quarter. Bulleted items outline what can be done to narrow unfavorable gaps.
- Highlights of key committee meetings.
- An analysis of nonperforming loans and trends in loan quality.
- Trend graphs that report profitability, credit quality, capital adequacy, productivity, and liquidity funding.

The chairman's report package is only 15 pages. If he wants details, they are only a phone call away. Questions have been anticipated by the preparers of the report.

Scan the chairman's desk further and you find a half full "in box." He encourages staff members to communicate by writing memos and only tell him what he needs to know. However, he emphasizes he doesn't like surprises. The staff concentrates on providing him with information that decreases risk and enhances the direction of business. They know what they are accountable for and inform him on those areas in clear, concise language.

In committee meetings, the staff's information-reporting attributes are similar. Staff members focus on summarizing decisions succinctly, hitting on only relevant issues. Here's a look at some of these committees.

Asset and Liability Committee (ALCO)—Its reports to senior management are easy to understand. ALCO members know how to simplify a complex subject to a format from which management can review, understand, and make decisions.

Loan Committee—Its members give directions using a variety of reports that tell them about loan quality by industry, location, and customer. They are aware of major factors affecting each sector.

Pricing Committee—It knows the unit cost and profitability of all products for which pricing decisions are made. The committee considers several factors in pricing, such as product profitability, corporate strategy on market presence, customer reaction, competition, and regulatory constraints. It has information to support the evaluation of each factor, drawing from a good cost accounting system.

First Performance Financial Institution as you see has a solid information-reporting philosophy. The institution emphasizes concise executive information and control reporting that entails the following:

- "In boxes" are not cluttered with nice-to-have information, and even need-to-know information, though emphasized, is limited.

- Information reporting is unified. Reports don't come from two areas reporting the same data.

- Information that management must know, such as exceptions in performance, is mentioned in the first paragraph of each report.

- When numbers are presented, the meaning is clear and obvious. Managers don't have to puzzle over meaning.

What Management Must Do

A vigorous leadership style is needed to produce a high-performance institution. A robust organization results from a purposeful and well-orchestrated management style. A nimble response is possible because adversity is rehearsed. The CEO knows what he wants to do in advance.

Top management moves the institution toward high performance by doing the following:

- Providing a clear message on the institution's goals and objectives.

- Establishing accountability for each staff member and measuring each person's performance.

- Emphasizing tactical and strategic planning. Inducing key managers to participate and buy into the process. Conveying a message that the plans are to be taken seriously.

- Insisting on concise and relevant information-and-control reporting. Eliminating internal junk mail.

- Insulating the institution from risk by having an effective risk-management-reporting program.
- Exuding an active marketing stance. Becoming a pricing leader. Finding a niche in the market that matches the institution's image.
- Eliminating unnecessary staff. Challenging future staff additions and replacements. Asking for justification of value added.
- Building a team. Inspiring the institution's staff to collaborate toward achieving the same goal.
- Focusing on the institution's customers, staff, profitability, risk, and performance.

All of these points are achievable. Some of them are short-term goals; others will take longer. The idea is to start now to breach the barriers to high performance.

The following is a self-analysis grid. It lets top management know where they are on the high-performance scale. All "yes" answers indicate the highest score possible.

Summary

High performance is achievable. It is made easier when data systems provide financial institutions with timely, reliable, and focused information. Management accounting eases the process.

High-Performance Self-Analysis Grid

	YES	NO

Clear Accountability

Everyone knows his or her purpose, goals, and objectives in the organization. ____ ____

There is no ambiguity about what is to be done, when it is to be done, and why. ____ ____

There are no competing departments within the bank. ____ ____

Open Communication

Managerial open-door policy. Employees have open access to management. ____ ____

Management receives no surprises. ____ ____

Each employee knows what his or her rated performance level is. ____ ____

Positive rewards are given frequently for superior and distinctive service. ____ ____

Actionable Strategy

Key managers meet off-site at least once a year to do strategic planning. ____ ____

The strategic plan has realistic action items that are closely monitored for progress by senior management. ____ ____

Key managers are aware of and committee to the strategic plan. ____ ____

The strategic plan integrates organization goals with products and customers. ____ ____

Concise Executive Information-and-Control Reporting

The chairman, CEO, and chief operating officer have timely and focused decision-information packages delivered to their offices. They are satisfied with the information they receive. It makes sense and is credible. ____ ____

Effective Risk Management

Information on risk is easy to read and understand. There are no blind spots. The following risk is reported: ____ ____

Credit risk ____ ____

Operating risk ____ ____

Interest rate risk ____ ____

Continued on next page

Planning

High-Performance Self-Analysis Grid (Continued)

	YES	NO
Capital risk	—	—
Liquidity risk	—	—
The bank knows where it is making money by:		
Organization	—	—
Product	—	—
Major customer	—	—

Active Marketing Stance

	YES	NO
Customers are important.	—	—
There is total customer-relationship reporting.	—	—
The financial institution has a clear, consistent, and positive image in the market.	—	—

Lean Team Approach

	YES	NO
The institution has four or fewer management layers.	—	—
There are fewer staff members to assets than most financial institutions.	—	—
Everyone keeps busy and is held accountable for specific results.	—	—
There are no vague or redundant departments. All departments provide a discernible and noncontroversial value-added service.	—	—

18

2
Strategic Planning

Planning is an essential and integral part of maintaining a healthy and viable organization. Planning helps an organization to formally declare its purpose, goals, and future actions.

Through proper planning, a chart of where the organization is headed and how it intends to get there is developed. It puts guidelines and controls on what will be done to accomplish goals.

This chapter discusses two kinds of planning—strategic and tactical. A strategic plan is more commonly known as a business plan and generally looks three to five years in the future. A tactical plan is more commonly known as an operating plan; it is designed for one year.

Integrating strategic and tactical planning is important. The normal process in a financial institution is to start the planning cycle with a strategic plan because it will serve as the basis for an operating plan.

Planning helps an institution toward a healthy posture as an organization and a provider of services. This chapter covers a basic 10-step planning process. In actual practice, the number of steps depends on individual preferences. Planning is usually conducted according to a management's style—the reason some institutions do more planning than others. Planning is a means of survival by providing a framework for measuring performance.

Concept of Planning

Planning Cycle

The planning cycle should begin in spring with a strategic business plan. This may reflect the results of a key management weekend planning retreat. The business plan is reviewed and revised. It contains narrative and quantitative data and usually is at a high-level summary.

Next, the institution engages in a preplanning process. The assumptions and numbers from the strategic business plan are further refined and applied to next year's plan. Senior management provides guidelines. This should be done in June. Armed with year-to-date actuals and plan variances, managers revise their outlook for the current year. Senior management reviews the pre plans and requests revisions.

In early fall, a detailed regular plan is put together. The preplan is used as a basis for constructing the regular plan. Management provides guidelines and objectives based on the business outlook. There may be a series of revisions as management strives for a plan that reflects profit objectives for the next year. The final plan is usually approved by the board in December. Planning forces key personnel to maintain a close sensitivity to events affecting profitability. The plan provides management with a hands-on control lever. A well-managed organization devotes significant resources toward planning, which fosters a discipline that leads to effective management.

Strategic Planning

As mentioned, the planning cycle begins with a strategic business plan. Usually an analyst gathers background data for planning. Background data include economic factors such as interest rates and inflation rates, both historical and forecasted. Information on regulatory issues, market share, products, and profitability also are gathered. Other data include a brief history of the organization and issues confronting it. All are summarized for senior management to review.

Next, a planning session is scheduled. It works best when conducted as a weekend retreat or some other off-site arrangement. The idea is to get away from the daily operations and focus on planning without interruption. The session is usually chaired by the CEO, who is assisted by a facilitator or coordinator. A consultant should be brought in to facilitate and structure the session. Key members of the management team are brought in to participate.

The management team reviews the research data and focuses on looking at the organization's position relative to strengths, weaknesses, opportunities, and threats (SWOT).

For example, SWOT questions include:

- **Strengths**—Where are the organization's strengths relative to:

  People?

  Organization Structure?

  Financial Condition?

  Products?

  Image?

  Market Presence?

- **Weaknesses**—Where are the organization's weaknesses relative to:

  People?

  Organization Structure?

  Financial Condition?

  Products?

  Image?

  Market Presence?

- **Opportunities**—Where are the organization's opportunities relative to:

  People?

  Organization Structure?

  Financial Condition?

Products?

Image?

Market Presence?

- **Threats**—Where are the organization's threats relative to:

People?

Organization Structure?

Financial Condition?

Products?

Image?

Market Presence?

Also maintained is a perspective on capital adequacy, asset quality, management effectiveness, earnings, and liquidity.

The CEO explains his or her ideas and those of the board. The stage is set for ideation and possibly time for generating free-form thinking. The CEO also shares his or her vision for the future—a statement of where the CEO and the board would like to see the organization several years from now.

A number of issues usually are raised on how the organization is going to fulfill its mission and put new ideas into action.

Line managers are challenged to develop business plans—with narrative and quantitative support. Their plans should talk about their respective business units and how they fit into the institution generally. They also discuss what changes they see as being necessary to fulfill the institution's long-term objectives. A general time table is outlined and relevant costs are quantified, if possible. The business plans extend three to five years in the future. Relevant revenue, expenses, balances, staff, and other factors are estimated. This is a high-level plan. Resources necessary to carry out the plan are mentioned. The rationalization and logic to support the plan are explained.

All of the business plans are analyzed and compared to the institution's overall strategic plan (see Figure 1). The idea is to ensure they conform with the organization's overall direction and objectives.

The idea of a strategic plan is to recognize some long-term issues that are important to the health and survival of the organization and to deal with those issues. This process usually takes place in the spring of each year. The strategic plan serves as a basis for the tactical (operating) plan.

The Steps of Strategic Planning

Step 1: Ideation

Step 1 of planning is ideation or generating ideas. Strategic planning begins with prompting top management team members to think about the organization's future. The CEO in conjunction with the board initiates the process. He or she may mention briefly some of the challenging issues he or she foresees in the institution's future. The top management team may be asked to think about these issues and others that may come to mind. This is a creativity exercise and the thinking process should be unstructured. This allows for unconventional solutions and ideas to surface. Team participants are asked to focus on the future. Through their creative thinking processes they are equipped to surface ideas that may develop into concrete strategies.

The ideas need not be formal; they may simply be expressed as penciled notes to take to the strategic planning retreat.

Step 2: Strategic Planning Retreat

A lot of logistical activity has to take place in preparing for the planning retreat. Often a planning coordinator or planning department does the preliminary research and gathers background information for the meeting. The research should focus on providing information relative to the following:

- Competition
- Regulatory
- Economic
- Customers
- Products
- Technology
- Organization
- Staff

Take each one and see what kind of information is needed.

Competition

- Who are the major competitors?
  (For each one explore the following.)
- What are their market strengths?
- What are their market weaknesses?
- What are their organizational strengths?
- What are their organizational weaknesses?
- How does their performance compare to our organization?
- Do they have a special niche in the marketplace?
- What is their market share?
- What surprises have come from their institution in the last year?
- Were we prepared to respond?
- What kinds of threats can we expect from them in the future?

Regulatory

- What are the regulations regarding:
  Geographic boundaries?
  Permissible lines of business?
  Capital requirements?
- What kinds of changes are possible in the future regarding:
  Geographic boundaries?
  Permissible lines of business?
  Capital requirements?

Economic

- What is the status and future outlook on world, national, regional, and local economies relative to:
  Inflation?
  Specific industries?

Economic conditions (expansion, stagnation, deceleration)?

- What is the status and future outlook on:

Interest rates?

Foreign exchange?

- How will these factors affect the institution?

Customers

What is our target customer, group, or groups?

Are we adequately focusing on them? (Are we providing the full range of products they need?)

What is our market share of the target customer?

What customers are most profitable to us?

What customers are least profitable to us?

What is a typical profile of our ideal customer?

What are the changes occurring in the marketplace that will affect our customer base?

Are we ignoring customer segments that could be served profitably?

Do we have adequate customer relationship information?

(Can we effectively manage key customer relationships?)

Products

What are our most profitable products?

What are our least profitable products?

What are the pressures for new products?

Is our organization developing new products to meet these forces?

Which products are being displaced?

Which products are forcing the most pressure on data processing, space, and staff? (Are the products profitable?)

Which products or subproducts pose the most risk?

Technology

What is the institution's need for technological upgrades in:
  Processing?
  Information?
What are the priorities requiring attention on:
  Threats?
  Opportunities?
What are the risks of:
  Proceeding with specific projects?
  Starting new projects?

Organization

Which profit centers are most profitable?
Which profit centers are least profitable?
What is the noninterest expense trend for the last five years?
What are the current plans for expansion, change, or contraction?
Are these plans consistent with customer targets and products offered?

Staff

What is the staff count trend for the last five years?
Are there any regulatory issues confronting the institution, such as Equal Employment Opportunity Commission (EEOC) issues?
What is the average age of the top officers and middle officers?
Does the organization have a succession plan?
What is the average for each staff on revenue, expense, assets, and deposits?
What is the annual turnover factor?
What are the major reasons for staff leaving the organization?
If turnover is high, how can it be lowered?

This background information should be given to the retreat participants before the meeting. The data will serve as reference material during the high-level planning discussions.

The retreat setting should be void of distractions. The atmosphere should be relaxed and conducive to an open exchange of ideas. Sometimes a consultant can be helpful as facilitator of the planning sessions. He or she can oftentimes break down communication barriers and help keep discussions on track.

Planning sessions in a retreat environment are useful in stimulating new ideas. The overall purpose should be to:

- Foster open communication.
- Identify and resolve major issues confronting the organization.
- Motivate managers to think creatively and come up with new ideas.

Several items should be discussed at the retreat sessions. Suggested agenda points for discussion include:

- What is our organization?
- What is our purpose, niche in the market?
- Why are we in business?
- Where is our organization today?
- What do we have to do to survive in the future?

The health of the organization and its business should be evaluated. The evaluation should include reviewing the organization's strengths, weaknesses, opportunities, and threats (SWOT). Look at this from four perspectives—organization, products, customers, and marketplace.

- **Strengths**
  Where is the organization considered a leader? (public image)
  Where is the organization considered strong by the public?

Does the institution have a strong organization with qualified people, workable chain of command, good communication, and effective business units?

Which products are paying for themselves?

With which customer base is the institution most strongly identified?

- Weaknesses

Where is the institution considered a follower by the public? (public image)

Where is the organization considered weak by the public?

What are the organizational weaknesses involving people, chain of command, communication, and business units?

Which products are not paying for themselves?

With which customer bases is the institution weakest? Are any of these segments current target markets? If so, what should be done to strengthen them?

- **Opportunities**

What are the market opportunities given current regulations and their future changes?

What are the market opportunities given technological changes?

What are the market opportunities given competitive changes?

What are the organizational opportunities given changes in business direction?

What are the profit improvement opportunities through pricing, A/L management, cost containment, and cost reduction?

- **Threats**

What are the market threats given current regulations and future changes?

What are the market threats given technological changes?

What are the market threats given product innovations?

What are the market threats given competitive changes?

What are the threats of risk in credit, liquidity, capital, and interest rates?

What are the organizational threats given changes in business direction?

The institution is dealing with uncertainty when it reviews opportunities and threats. Consequently, management should develop some high-level "what-if" scenarios. The question list can be lengthy, so the meeting's facilitator has to choose questions pertinent to the institution's environment.

Planning sessions should result in:

- A mission statement, briefly telling the organization's purpose and broad business direction.
- An outline of broad goals and objectives.
- An action list that says how to handle major issues confronting the institution.
- A list of selected business targets, including geographic, product, and organizational matters involving mergers, acquisitions, start-ups.
- A broad policy statement and contingency plan covering risks.
- A decision on how to measure productivity in selected areas using key performance indicators (KPIs).
- A list of priorities.
- A top-level strategic plan outline.

Step 3: Prepare a Strategic Plan

This step involves the major business units and takes place in March or April after the planning retreat. The results of the planning retreat are communicated to middle management. In this step, the broad direction handed down by top management is translated into plans for specific business units.

If an institution is market driven, management will look first at the marketplace and the kinds of customers it wishes to serve.

This research will be translated into products that best serve the customers. Management then will look at the organizational and logistical support necessary to deliver the products. This action is a stark contrast to institutions that are only organizationally driven. They prepare business plans based solely on organizational considerations and agenda but largely ignore market forces. Such an organization tries to succeed on its organizational agenda and may suffer from inertia and have difficulty surviving.

The strategic planning step focuses on what must be done, how to do it, and what resources are required.

Several kinds of high-level strategic business plans have to be prepared, including:

- Market plan
- Product plan
- Operating plan
- Organizational plan

If the organization bases its plan on a market-driven philosophy, the market plan should be prepared first and coordinated with the other plans. These plans reach out three to five years.

- **Market Plan**

  This plan focuses on market opportunities, market share, and market segmentation. Using these factors and action items, a plan is prepared. It also should conform to the broad goals and objectives set by top management.

- **Product Plan**

  The product plan should use segments of the market plan and action items from the strategic plan as its basis. The product plan also should conform to the broad goals and objectives outlined by top management.

- **Operating Plan**

  The operating plan has four segments: analysis, strategy, action items, and financial projections. The segments are done by each strategic business unit on the following:

Balance sheet, if applicable

Revenue, if applicable

Expenses

Capital expenditures

Risk

- **Contingency Plans**

Data processing disaster recovery

Funding crisis

Management succession

Organizational crisis and resulting publicity

Step 3 constitutes strategic business plans for the major departmental units and a consolidated strategic plan for the institution.

Step 4: Executive Committee Review

The executive committee goes over the strategic plan in April or May. This top-management process includes a comprehensive look at the business-unit plans and the consolidated plan. The plans then are presented to the board of directors.

During the review process revisions may be made. However, the net result of Step 4 should be an approved strategic plan. From it come revised goals and objectives for use in the next preplan.

Writing the Strategic Plan

The strategic plan should be a high-level action-motivating document that deals broadly with issues. Objectives should have tolerance ranges. For example, an ROA objective should be set with a range of, say, 0.75 to 1.25 percent.

A three- or five-year strategic plan may contain the following:

- Preamble and CEO's overview

    - Explains broadly why the institution exists, what its mission and charter are.

- Explains what the plan represents.
- Tells how the plan relates to the short-term operating plan.
- Tells what is in the plan.
- Tells why the plan is important, e.g., rapid industry change.
- Explains key issues that have been ascertained and what they mean.
- Preface
  - Tells what the plan covers and what it doesn't.
  - Mentions planning time horizon.
- Overall corporate mission and charter
  - Declares the corporate mission succinctly.
  - Recaps the institution's charter in support of mission statement.
  - Sets forth corporation's basic beliefs on human resources, quality, growth, and other business factors.
- Profile of corporation's status and major issues
  - Reviews where the institution is today and covers the major issues confronting it.
  - Identifies the institution's strengths, weaknesses, opportunities, and threats. Emphasizes key capabilities. Assesses environmental considerations as they pertain to the organization.
  - Relates economic assumptions.
  - Considers regulatory and legislative matters, for example: deposit insurance, interstate banking, deregulation, tax reform, and capital adequacy.
  - Reviews competition for each business sector.
  - Makes driving-force statement about customers and products.
  - Addresses meeting the market's needs.

- Corporate goals and objectives statement
  - Tells future strategic profile and stance.
  - Predicts range of specific ratios and other measurable results to be achieved over a specified time. Ratios include ROA, ROE, equity, leverage, total capital to assets, asset growth, core deposits to funding, loans to assets, off-balance sheet financing, etc.
  - Lists action items required to attain objectives.
  - States goals/objectives for each strategic business unit.
- Corporate strategy and assumptions
  - Tell what the organization plans to do in the future and how it will do it.
  - List necessary steps for the corporation and each strategic business unit to attain achievement.
  - Lists high-level financial goals for the corporation and its strategic business units for the next three to five years.
  - Outline long-term and short-term strategy for:
    —Asset/liability management
    —Capital adequacy.
    —Staff development.
    —Corporate survival and excellenceechnology.
    —Revenue
    —Expenses
    —Balances
    —Market products and image

General Comments on Strategic Planning

Quality

In addition to comparing your institution to other high-performing institutions, also look at well-managed businesses outside of the financial services industry. Look for well-managed organizations regardless of industry. What are they doing that makes them good?

Organizations that emphasize good customer relations at all levels and in all products and services are likely to exercise higher quality. Even noncustomer-contact jobs should emphasize customer importance.

Risk

Plan for risk. Rehearse how to minimize injury to earnings from the following risks:

- Inflation
- Interest rates
- Exchange rates
- Credit
- Country (political and economic)
- Industry
- Customer
- Liquidity
- Fiduciary
- Operating
- Capital

An active plan can insulate your institution from these risks. Keep high standards and maintain policy benchmarks that prevent your organization from falling into short-term inducements that compromise your principles. Plan for steady long-term profits.

Be cautious and don't venture far from your area of expertise. Be careful about diversification.

When extending credit do not sacrifice quality for short-term bursts in profits. Maintain a strong, central control on credit quality. Stimulate and reward officers for loan quality as opposed to rewards for building loan volume, fees, and risky yields. A number of financial institutions are probably in trouble because of greed that wrought irrational decisions. They lost their reference point.

Overall Plan

- Establishes accountability for measurable results.
- Keeps a large focus on the future. Uses the past only as a reference point. Looks to future opportunities.
- Focuses on market potential.
- Keeps the plan simple, realistic, and practical.
- Stimulates plans that get action.

Summary

Strategic planning has four steps (see Figure 1). It involves (1) generating ideas, (2) holding planning sessions, (3) preparing business plans, and (4) conducting an executive committee review. The process should begin in January and end in May. Strategic planning sets the stage for tactical planning.

The strategic plan is long term and sets forth what the institution's purposes are for the future. It must be realistic and attainable to be effective. Managers also must be able to identify with the plan so they can specify actions necessary to accomplish the objectives.

Strategic planning is long term because it is directed toward organizational survival and issues needing a lot of lead time.

Figure 1
Key Steps to Strategic Planning in Financial Institutions

Planning Steps	Strategic			
	1	**2**	**3**	**4**
	Ideation	**Strategic Planning Retreat**	**Major Units Prepare Strategic Business Plans**	**Executive Committee Review**
Time Table	January-February	March	March-April	April-May
Management Participants	Top management team members (individual process)	Top management team members	Middle management	Top management
Tasks	• Creative thinking • Vision for future	• Review factors impacting institution • Establish priorities • Establish broad goals and objectives	• Translate goals and objectives into strategic plans	• Review business plans • Review consolidated plan • Present to board
Deliverables	• Ideas	• Top level strategic plan outline	• Major units' strategic business plans • Consolidated strategic plan	• Revisions, approvals, and direction

3
Tactical Planning and Budgeting

Tactical planning provides continuity and follow-up to strategic planning. The six-step process begins in June of each year. It starts with a high-level preplan that must conform to the recently formulated strategic plan. The preplans are reviewed in July by top management.

After these reviews, top management holds a retreat with key middle managers and discusses goals and objectives. They solicit ideas. These ideas and the feedback on preplan submissions set the stage for the regular plan. A preplan is prepared by all responsibility center managers who participate in the regular plan. This session occurs in late August. The regular plans will serve as next year's operating plan.

Plan reviews begin in October. They result in revisions, approvals, and further direction. There may be several revisions during these reviews. The last step is a presentation of the plan for board approval in December.

The main areas of tactical planning include balance sheet planning, expense planning, and capital expenditures budgeting.

The Tactical Planning and Budgeting Process

The tactical plan is a one-year operating plan, which draws action items from strategic plans. If strategic planning is taken seriously and the institution's management is intent on change, a host of action items used in the tactical plan will be derived from the strategic plan.

If the business unit preparing a tactical plan is a profit center, projections on business activity, revenue, expense, and balances (if any) are prepared. The business environment is reconciled to the strategic plan objectives. Usually the CEO issues tactical planning objectives resulting from the strategic planning exercise. Assuming the institution is growing, the objectives are usually broad and cover:

- Revenue growth
- Expense growth
- Balanced growth
- ROA
- ROE
- Full-time-equivalent (FTE) staff

Each business unit manager should fill out a plan (budget) package. It is usually a collection of forms, which in most institutions reflect month-by-month entries. The outlook for the current year also is projected from what has occurred year-to-date.

The preplan is a high-level summary, as contrasted to a detailed plan, and does not get into specific monthly line item projections. The preplan may include line item projections for the next year. Mostly, it shows how the business unit manager plans to conform to the CEO's objectives for next year. It contains relevant revenue, expense, balance, and activity projections.

The preplan is reviewed and revised when necessary. Next comes the regular tactical planning that may begin in early fall. Several passes or revisions may be made and the process could continue into December, when the board usually approves the final version of the plan.

A question arises: Is that all a financial institution does is plan? The answer is yes and no. Yes, planning is almost an annual duration cycle. No, planning doesn't require a business unit manager's undivided attention during the cycle. Planning that we discuss here provides management with budgetary control tools. It gives managers the necessary information to discern what is reasonable and expected.

Parallel to tactical planning is capital budgeting. Capital budgeting is planning for expenditures on items that will be capitalized rather than expensed.

Examples include purchases of equipment and automobiles; leasehold improvements; owned property improvements; construction of new facilities; and land purchases. Several factors are to be considered here. One is the cash-flow implications. Another is taxation on capital purchases or improvements. All have to be reviewed during this budgeting process. The larger the institution, the more likely it will have a capital budgeting package that consists of instructions and forms. The package helps the institution plan and control capital expenditures for next year. The forms sometimes include a depreciation schedule to give the business unit manager the opportunity to calculate the depreciation expense attributable to capital purchases and/or improvements.

As a corporate issue, a lease-versus-buy analysis usually takes place before purchases are made.

Step 1: Preliminary Plan

This step begins the tactical planning process. Tactical planning has a one-year horizon. The process begins in June or July with a preliminary plan (preplan). The preplan draws heavily from the recently completed and reviewed strategic plan. The preplan also uses the current year's operating plan and year-to-date results as a reference point.

A preplan is prepared for each responsibility center (RC). The result is a revised forecast for this year and a high-level preliminary plan for next year.

Step 2: Preliminary Plan Reviews

This step involves top management. The managers review the preplans for consistency with the institution's goals, objectives, and guidelines. This occurs in July.

The result of this step is clarification on goals and objectives through preplan revisions. The preplan for the institution is approved and further direction is given to the strategic business units and their responsibility centers.

Step 3: Planning Retreat

The planning retreat could be in July. It is a time for top management to meet with key middle managers. The purpose is to discuss top-level refinements needed from the preplan to conform to next year's goals and objectives. These are discussed and top management strives to get middle managers to buy into the goals. Resources necessary to achieve them are explored.

Four things should be accomplished in this meeting:

- Goals and objectives are clarified.
- Top management relates broad direction on how to achieve them.
- New ideas from middle management are discussed.
- Middle managers buy into goals and objectives.

Step 4: Regular Plan

Some call the regular plan the financial or operating plan. It is next year's plan. This step occurs in late August and September. It involves all responsibility-center (RC) managers. They prepare a detailed month-by-month plan for next year. They also revise estimates for the current year. Depending on whether the RC is a profit or cost center, a lending or deposit gathering unit, detailed budget information is developed for next year by the RC manager that includes:

- Balance sheet
- Revenue
- Expense
- Capital expenditures

On the corporate level additional plans may be developed and possibly would include the following:

- Tax plan

- Capital plan
- Cash flow plan

Step 5: Plan Reviews

Regular operating plans are reviewed and revised in October and November. Several interchanges may take place between top and middle management. Several revisions may occur during these reviews.

Top management reviews the plans for consistency with the strategic plan and next year's goals, objectives, and guidelines.

The result should be an operating plan that top management is comfortable enough with to recommend to the board for approval.

Step 6: Presentation to the Board

The directors review the plan in December. Because they have been involved in setting goals, objectives, and guidelines for next year, there should be no big surprises. The plan should essentially conform to their earlier expectations.

Revisions could arise from this review, necessitated by internal and external changes.

If there were a step 7, it would be "measure plan to actual." For planning to be effective, results must be measured. Performance reporting does this for management. This helps management to maintain a results-driven posture. Such things as key performance indicators (KPIs) are reviewed for each strategic business unit (SBU). KPIs should be planned so management can evaluate performance against plan.

Balance Sheet Planning

The balance sheet plan serves as a basis for determining the planned gross-interest income, cost of funds, net-interest income, loan-loss provision, and changes in the balance sheet mix.

The balance sheet plan should be arranged to accommodate sensitivity of what-if kinds of analysis. This allows management to

41

simulate several scenarios and determine the potential impact of decisions before they happen.

In balance sheet planning, the first step is to categorize the planning items according to sources and uses of funds.

Here is a summary of the composition of sources:

- Customer-based funds
- Market-based funds
- Long-term debt and capital leases
- Noninterest-bearing funds
- Equity

A summary on the composition of uses:

- Loans ad leases
- Investment securities
- Time deposits placed
- Other earning assets
- Other assets

The institution's current balance sheet is the starting point. For each source of the fund's (liabilities and capital) balance category, a cost of funds is calculated, where applicable. This is predicated on developing a derived-average cost of funds, where applicable. It requires interest rate assumptions where interest rate scenarios become useful.

The present balance sheet composition for the funds using side (assets) also is used as a starting point. Gross anticipated interest income is calculated for each asset category. Again, interest rate assumptions are used.

The current net interest income is derived by subtraction as is net yield.

At this point, some institutions would go one more step and calculate a loan-loss provision for each loan category.

In the planning cycle, each forecast is driven by a set of assumptions developed from the strategic business plan and the institution's current outlook.

In planning for balances you need to consider:

Assets

- Funding constraints
- Capital constraints
- Credit risk
- Interest-rate risk
- New business
- Loan amortization
- Prepayments
- Target market
- Target products
- Liquidity requirements

Liabilities and Equity

- Funding requirements
- Liquidity risk
- Interest rates
- New products
- Target markets
- Capital requirements
- Maturity gaps

The asset/liability management committee should be active in balance-sheet planning processes.

Figure 2 is an example of a balance sheet plan:

This balance sheet is for the total institution. It summarizes all its organizations. The asset, liability, and equity categories listed also are at a high-level summary. There should be a peel-back balance sheet that shows more categories and, hence, provides more details.

Figure 2
XYZ Financial Institution
Balance Sheet Plan

Balances ($ in 000's)

Category	J	F	M	A	M	J	J	A	S	O	N	D	Total Average Next Year's Plan	Total Estimated Average This Year	Total Average Plan This Year	Total Average Last Year
• Assets																
Cash and Due from Banks	1,500	1,500	1,600	1,700	1,700	1,700	1,700	1,700	1,700	1,700	1,700	1,700	1,658	1,550	1,500	1,400
Time Deposits Placed	2,700	2,800	2,800	2,800	2,900	2,900	3,000	3,000	3,100	3,100	3,100	3,100	2,941	2,500	2,300	2,200
Investment and Trading Securities	3,400	3,400	3,400	3,400	3,400	3,500	3,500	3,500	3,500	3,500	3,500	3,500	3,458	3,300	3,200	3,000
Loans	8,000	8,100	8,200	8,300	8,300	8,400	8,400	8,500	8,500	8,600	8,800	9,000	8,417	7,700	7,500	7,000
Leases	400	400	400	400	500	500	500	500	500	500	500	500	467	350	350	300
Customers' Acceptance Liability	650	700	700	800	800	800	800	800	800	800	800	800	771	625	630	600
Other Assets	1,600	1,600	1,650	1,700	1,700	1,700	1,700	1,700	1,700	1,700	1,700	1,700	1,679	1,575	1,550	1,500
Premises	700	700	700	700	700	700	700	700	700	700	700	700	700	700	700	650
Total	$18,950	19,200	19,450	19,800	20,000	20,100	20,300	20,400	20,500	20,600	20,800	21,000	20,091	18,300	17,730	16,650

Figure 2 (Continued)

Balances
($ in 000's)

Category	J	F	M	A	M	J	J	A	S	O	N	D	Total Average Next Year's Plan	Total Estimated Average This Year	Total Average Plan This Year	Total Average Last Year
• Liabilities and Equity																
Deposits																
Demand (noninterest)	3,400	3,400	3,400	3,500	3,500	3,500	3,500	3,600	3,600	3,600	3,600	3,600	3,516	3,300	3,200	3,100
Savings and NOW Accounts	4,100	4,100	4,200	4,300	4,300	4,300	4,400	4,400	4,500	4,500	4,600	4,500	4,350	4,000	3,900	3,700
Time	8,000	8,100	8,200	8,300	8,400	8,400	8,400	8,400	8,700	8,700	8,700	8,700	8,416	7,800	7,800	7,400
Borrowed Funds	1,646	1,746	1,796	1,743	1,843	1,943	2,037	2,037	1,737	1,830	1,930	2,230	1,877	1,451	1,076	849
Acceptances Outstanding	650	700	700	800	800	800	800	800	800	800	800	800	771	625	630	600
Other	270	270	270	270	270	270	270	270	270	270	270	270	270	270	270	270
Shareholders' Equity	884	884	884	887	887	887	893	893	893	900	900	900	891	854	854	731
Total	$18,950	19,200	19,450	19,800	20,000	20,100	20,300	20,400	20,500	20,600	20,800	21,000	20,091	18,300	17,730	16,650

Four risks must be considered in balance sheet planning. They are credit risk, interest-rate risk, liquidity risk, and capital adequacy risk.

The balance sheet must conform to the strategic plan's goals and objectives. Goals such as growth, capital adequacy, and product emphasis must be considered.

A month-by-month listing and trend analysis are important for a detailed plan. Figure 2 shows January through December, plus a trend analysis. The trend analysis includes the total planned average balances by category for next year, the total estimated actual average for the current year, the total average balances planned for the current year, and the total average balances for last year.

In planning a balance sheet, there has to be a "plug" category for assets and one for liabilities to ensure they are balanced. On the asset side for surplus funds, the default category is cash and due from banks (funds placed). The default category on the liability side for funding shortages is borrowed funds.

Revenue Planning

Three sources of revenue exist in a revenue plan. They are (1) fee revenue, (2) net interest income, and (3) other income.

Fee Revenue. Fee revenue is planned based on the following considerations:

- Volume
- Pricing
- New products
- Products to be discontinued

A specific plan should be developed for each major product line. Some financial institutions even prepare a projected profit and loss statement for each major product line and integrate it into the overall planning process.

Net Interest Income. Interest rates are applied against the balance sheet module to arrive at gross interest income and cost of funds. Loan fees and amortizations must be considered in the yield calculations for loans.

Net interest income is derived using the following formula:

Net interest income = Gross interest income – Cost of funds

Other Income. This income comes from a variety of sources. You must distinguish income from continuing sources (operating income) and income from unusual sources (nonoperating income).

Figure 3 is an example of total institution income from the three sources of fee revenue, net interest income, and other income.

There should be a peel-back plan that shows the details of the revenue for each product. Each should elaborate assumptions and show the necessary calculations. A 12-month trend analysis should be provided in the revenue plan.

Expense Planning

Expense planning encompasses all noninterest expenses. These include staff compensation expense and other operating expenses. Including staff counts as part of the compensation planning is important.

The following items are considered in expense planning:

- Staffing
  - Full-time equivalent staff
- Compensation expense
  - Regular salaries
  - Overtime
  - Bonuses and incentives
  - Employee benefits
  - Agency and temporary
- Other operating expenses
  - Marketing and advertising
  - Entertainment

Figure 3
XYZ Financial Institution
Revenue Planning Example

($ in 000's)
Revenue from Fee-Based Services
Other Income and Net Interest Income

Fee and Other Categories	J	F	M	A	M	J	J	A	S	O	N	D	Total Next Year's Plan	Total Estimated Actual This Year	Total Plan This Year	Total Actual Last Year
Fee Revenue																
• Trust Fees	$2	3	2	4	2	2	1	2	2	2	3	2	$27	$24	$23	$20
• Service Charges on Deposit Accounts	3	3	3	3	2	2	3	3	3	2	2	3	32	28	27	24
• Factoring Commissions	1	1	1	2	2	1	1	1	1	1	1	1	14	10	9	9
• Safe Deposit Rent	1	1	1	1	2	1	1	1	1	1	1	1	12	10	9	9
• Merchant Discount Fees	1	1	1	1	1	1	1	1	1	1	2	3	15	13	12	11
• Bank Card Fees	1	1	1	1	1	1	1	1	1	1	3	3	16	12	11	10
Other Income																
• Trading Account Profits and Fees	1	2	1	3	1	1	2	1	1	1	2	1	17	14	13	12
• Foreign Exchange Income	1	1	1	1	1	1	1	1	1	1	1	1	12	9	9	8
• Bankers' Acceptances	1	1	1	1	1	2	1	2	2	1	2	2	18	15	14	13
• Letters of Credit	3	2	2	2	2	2	2	2	2	2	2	2	25	23	22	20
• Miscellaneous Income	1	1	1	1	1	1	1	1	1	1	1	2	13	8	8	8
Subtotal	16	17	15	21	15	15	15	16	16	14	20	21	201	166	157	144
• Net Interest Income*	42	43	44	45	45	47	47	45	46	48	49	49	550	524	512	500
Total Revenue	58	60	59	66	60	62	62	61	62	62	69	70	751	690	669	644

* From earning assets after loan-loss provisions. Includes loan fees. Information is from balance sheet module.

- – Travel
- – Professional and community
- – Contributions
- – Recruiting
- – Subscriptions
- – Postage and delivery
- – Stationery and supplies
- – Telephone
- – Data processing
- – Equipment maintenance
- – Equipment rent
- – Insurance
- – Legal
- – Premises (occupancy)
- – Consulting
- – Service charges
- – Miscellaneous
- – Depreciation
- • Expense transfers (department to department)
  - – Incoming transfers
  - – Outgoing transfers

Figure 4 is an example of a summarized total institution-level expense plan.

Each responsibility center (RC) should submit an expense plan.

The next schedule (Figure 5) is used for top management presentation. It condenses each major plan element such as revenue and expense into a single line. The schedule provides a brief overview that can be compared against high-level objectives.

Figure 4
XYZ Financial Institution
Expense Planning Example

($ in 000's)
Staff Equivalencies, Compensation Expense, and
Other Operating Expense

Categories	J	F	M	A	M	J	J	A	S	O	N	D	Total Next Year's Plan	Total Estimated Actual This Year	Total Plan This Year	Total Actual Last Year
Staff Count																
Average Equivalent	19.0	19.0	20.0	20.0	20.0	20.0	20.0	19.0	19.0	19.0	19.0	20.0	19.5	18.0	17.0	15.4
December Equivalent	-	-	-	-	-	-	-	-	-	-	-	-	20.0	19.0	17.0	16.0
Compensation Expense																
Salaries	32	32	34	34	34	34	34	32	32	32	32	38	$400	$366	$306	$231
Overtime	2	1	1	1	1	1	1	1	1	1	2	2	15	11	12	10
Benefits	6	6	7	7	7	7	7	6	6	6	6	9	80	69	55	40
Total	40	39	42	42	42	42	42	39	39	39	40	49	$495	$446	$373	$281
Other Operating Expense																
Marketing and Advertising	1	1	1	1	1	1	0	0	1	1	1	1	10	10	10	7
Premises	5	5	5	5	5	5	6	6	6	6	6	6	66	60	55	34
Equipment Rent	3	3	3	3	3	3	3	3	3	4	4	4	38	35	27	18
Data Processing	1	1	1	1	1	1	1	1	0	1	1	1	11	4	4	13
Insurance	0	0	2	0	0	2	0	0	3	0	0	3	10	10	10	10
Entertainment	.2	.2	.2	.1	0	0	0	0	0	0	0	0	.7	.7	.7	.7
Transportation and Travel	1.4	1.4	1.4	1.4	1.4	1.4	1.4	1.4	1.4	1.4	1.4	1.4	16.8	6.8	8.0	1.0

Figure 4 (Continued)

($ in 000's)

Staff Equivalencies, Compensation Expense, and Other Operating Expense

Categories	J	F	M	A	M	J	J	A	S	O	N	D	Total Next Year's Plan	Total Estimated Actual This Year	Total Plan This Year	Total Actual Last Year
Other Operating Expense (Continued)																
Professional and Community	0	0	.3	0	0	0	0	0	.2	0	0	.6	1.1	1.1	1.0	1.0
Contributions	0	0	0	0	0	0	0	0	0	0	0	.3	.3	.3	1.0	1.0
Recruiting	0	0	0	.5	0	0	0	0	0	0	.4	0	.9	.9	2.0	1.0
Subscriptions	0	0	.2	0	0	.2	0	0	0	0	0	.8	1.2	1.2	2.0	1.0
Postage and Delivery	1.8	.8	.8	.8	.8	.8	.8	1.8	.8	.8	1.8	.8	12.6	12.6	15.0	8.0
Stationery and Supplies	.5	.5	.5	.5	1.2	.5	.5	.5	.5	1.5	.5	.5	7.7	7.7	10.0	9.0
Telephone	1	1	1	1	1	1	1	1	1	1	1	1	12.0	12.0	13.0	6.0
Equipment Maintenance	.1	.1	.1	.1	1.1	.1	.1	.1	1.1	.1	1.1	.1	4.2	4.2	6.0	3.0
Legal	0	0	0	.5	0	1	0	0	0	1.5	0	0	3.0	3.0	3.0	3.0
Consulting	.3	0	1	.2	0	0	1	0	0	0	0	1	3.5	3.5	3.5	3.5
Service Charges	.2	0	0	0	0	0	0	.3	0	0	0	0	.5	.5	.5	.5
Depreciation	.5	.5	.5	.5	.5	.5	.5	.5	.5	.5	.5	.5	6.0	6.0	6.0	6.0
Miscellaneous	1	1.5	0	.4	0	.5	.7	.4	.5	.2	.3	0	5.5	4.5	12.3	5.3
Total	17	16	18	16	16	18	16	16	19	18	19	22	211	184	236	138
Total Expenses	57	55	60	58	58	60	58	55	58	57	59	71	706	630	563	419

Figure 5
XYZ Financial Institution
Net Income before Taxes

($ in 000s)

	J	F	M	A	M	J	J	A	S	O	N	D	Total Next Year's Plan	Total Estimated Actual This Year	Total Plan This Year	Total Actual Last Year
Revenue	$58	60	59	66	60	62	62	61	62	62	69	70	751	690	669	644
Expense	$57	55	60	58	58	60	58	55	58	57	59	71	706	630	563	419
Net Income before Taxes	$1	5	(1)	8	2	2	4	6	4	5	10	(1)	45	60	106	225

Pre-tax Earnings by Quarter

	First Quarter	Second Quarter	Third Quarter	Fourth Quarter
	$5	$12	$14	$14
Earnings per share	$0.21	$0.50	$0.58	$0.58

Capital Expenditures Budgeting

Capital expenditures budgeting is an important part of planning. Anything intended to be acquired or constructed and, hence, capitalized in the next year should be in the plan. Included are the following:

- Leasehold improvements
- Owned property improvements
- Acquisition of capital assets

An example of a leasehold improvement would be remodeling leased office space.

An example of owned property improvements would be vacant land owned by the institution slated as a construction site.

The intent of capital budgeting is to ensure that capital improvements and purchases are coordinated and controlled. Management thus can keep track of large fund outflows and their effect on future earnings by way of depreciation.

Capital expenditures budgeting should include a lease/buy analysis. The tax ramifications of each option should be explored. All budgeted capital expenditures should be summarized for top management to review.

Each responsibility center manager requesting a capital expenditure should have to fill out a capital budget form.

Figures 6 and 7 are examples of a capital budget form and a capital expenditures budget form.

This kind of a form forces the RC manager to fill out the budget carefully in evaluating his or her request. A concise estimate also is made on when the action will occur and how much will be spent. Additionally, justification for the planned expenditure is requested. RC managers also should supply backup details when necessary.

The CFO may opt to perform a lease/buy analysis on capital purchases such as computers and automobiles. Also, the CFO should perform a cost/benefit analysis on major projects to determine whether the projects are economically justified.

Figure 6
Capital Budget and Depreciation Schedule

Responsibility Center Name: Chief Financial Officer
Responsibility Center Number: 28750
Responsibility Center Manager: Ann Doe

Month of Expenditure Amount

Capital Expenditure	J	F	M	A	M	J	J	A	S	O	N	D	Total
AMB Computer	$6,500												6,500
Total													6,500
Depreciation													

Amount less salvage divided by useful life (expressed in months) (useful life guidelines are provided by CFO)

$6,500 − 0 = $6,500 ÷ 60 months = 108.33 per month

$108.33 x 12 months for next year = $1,300

Justification: CFO has an outdated computer. It is slow and has small storage space. Computer would enhance process through increased turnaround. It will save 2,000 hours of staff time per year.

Figure 7
XYZ Financial Institution
Capital Expenditures Budget

Capital Expenditure	Amount	Annual Depreciation Expense	Depreciation Years	R.C. No.	Location	Justification of Need
Leasehold Improvements	$10,000	$ 667	15	35782	4th Street branch	Installation of drive-up machine for motor banking
AMB Computer	6,500	1,300	5	28750	CFO—Headquarters	Needed for planning
Totals	$16,500	1,967				

R.C. No. = Responsibility Center Number.

Capital budgeting is a powerful management tool used for initiating, evaluating, and controlling capital expenditures. A budget also can ensure that outlays aren't at cross purposes with the institution's strategy.

All major projects should be monitored for progress and conformity. Upon completion, an analysis should be made to determine performance against budget. On a corporate level the CFO and a designated committee have the duty to recognize and evaluate capital investment opportunities. They also should evaluate and set priorities on requests from RC managers. The evaluation should consider the following factors:

- Urgency of need

- Cost

- Conformity to strategic plan

- Duration, if it is a project

- Risk, if it is a project

- Pay back

- Expected value

- Benefits

- Return on investment

Based on the foregoing, the committee will assign priorities and make recommendations. Some proposals will require extensive financial assessment before approval.

Summary

Planning is important in maintaining a viable and healthy organization. Planning provides a basis for controlling the organization's direction.

Tactical planning (Figure 8) derives its energy and direction from the strategic plan and translates long-term purposes into shot-term actions needed to accomplish those purposes.

For planning to be effective, all levels of management must be committed to it. A plan must be realistic, achievable, and understandable. High-performing financial institutions adhere to a well-defined planning cycle. They use it as a control tool and as a means to direct their future effectively.

Figure 8
Key Steps to Tactical Planning in Financial Institutions

	Tactical					
Planning Steps	**1 Preplan**	**2 Preplan Reviews**	**3 Planning Retreat**	**4 Regular Plan**	**5 Plan Reviews**	**6 Presentation to Board**
Time Table	June-July	July	July	August-September	October-November	December
Management Participants	All managers	Top management	Top management and key middle managers	All managers	Top and middle management	Top management
Tasks	• Prepare next year's operating plan (high-level).	• Review preplans for consistency with goals, objectives, and guidelines.	• Discuss goals and objectives	• Prepare next year's operating plan (detailed).	• Review plans for consistency with goals, objectives, and guidelines.	• Finalize and present plan to board.
Deliverables	• Next year's operating preplan	• Revisions, approvals, and direction	• Ideas	• Operating plans	• Revisions, approvals, and direction	• Final plan

Part II

Management Control

4

The Management Information Reporting Systems

Considerable amounts of information that go to the board of directors, chief executive officer (CEO), and chief operating officer (COO) come from the chief financial officer (CFO). The CFO serves as an official monitor of performance and compliance for many vital functions in an institution. Typically, the CFO is the driving force in developing a management information system for senior management.

Most CEOs and COOs view themselves as accountable to the board and stockholders for planning and policy, performance, and risk management. Risk can suddenly catch senior managers by surprise if their management information reporting system (MIRS) is inadequate.

This chapter is designed to assist the CEO, COO, and CFO in sorting out major risks and concerns and translate them into reporting requirements. The goal of this chapter is to provide a senior manager with tools on what to specify in developing an action oriented and responsive management information reporting system.

An Overview of Management Information Reporting

An institution's top management needs information that is timely, accurate, relevant, focused, and easy to understand. Also, there should be no unreported risks.

Building a management information reporting system that will service the needs of everyone isn't easy. But it is possible and practical to build one that leaves no major information gaps. Two kinds of gaps can exist. One is the gap between what a manager needs to fulfill his or her accountabilities and what is available. The other gap is what a manager would like to have and what is available.

The first gap is shown by the following example:

Information Need	Information Available	Information Gap
Loan Quality Ratings	None	Quality Ratings

A comprehensive list of information of what management could ask regarding credit risk is provided later in this chapter. In this example management needs to know more information about the institution's loan portfolio. Loan quality ratings are nonexistent. This gap needs to be addressed as management specifies information requirements for an MIRS.

The second gap, nice-to-have information, is illustrated by the example below:

Information Want	Information Available	Information Gap
Statistical Correlation Analysis between Loan Quality Ratings and Day of the Week Loans Were Booked.	Day of the Week Loans Were Booked.	Loan Quality and Correlation.

The first gap is illustrated by the following example:

Need: Credit Quality Information

- Delinquent Loans by Sector of Risk
- Credit Ratings by Sector of Risk
- Delinquent Loan Aging by Sector of Risk
  Sectors include:
    Industry
    Country/Geographic Location

What is available:

- Total Delinquent Loans (No Break-out)

Gap:

- Delinquent Loans by Sector of Risk
- Credit Ratings by Sector of Risk
- Delinquent Loan Aging by Sector of Risk

This second example, correlation of loan quality ratings with the day of the week loans were booked, shows an obviously unnecessary information specification. But these kinds of data are sometimes requested when you survey potential recipients of MIRS. But the requirements are withdrawn frequently when key questions are asked:

- What do you plan to do with this information?
- How will it help you to manage better?
- Are you willing to absorb the cost of producing this kind of information?

This kind of gap doesn't have to be filled. Nice-to-have information has a tendency to clutter an MIRS and also can be time consuming and costly to compile. What management needs is basic information that will help it oversee its accountabilities.

Determining Information Requirements

One of the most time-consuming processes is getting people to agree on what they need. Hours of interviewing and filling out questionnaires can be avoided by working from a generic, critical-success-factors list and translating it into information requirements.

Start with the board, CEO, and COO. As mentioned before, they are interested in monitoring planning and policy, performance, and risk management.

Their information needs are most likely at a high summary level and they may only want overview information on a regular basis. However, they may want access to details when interest in a particular subject arises. Obviously, managers reporting to top management and the board would need detailed information.

In Chapter 7, several management control formats will be presented. However, this chapter focuses on requirements and discusses how information is extracted and developed.

Let's take each management accountability and put more specific requirements with it.

- Planning and policy compliance
  - Strategic planning objectives fulfillmen.
  - Budget to actual compliance.
  - Operational policy, for example, lending limitsPersonnel policy, for example, merit increases in salaries.

Some managers view planning-target attainment and compliance as important measures. They may, however, feel that only policy compliance exceptions, i.e., noncompliance, should be called to their attention.

- Performance
  - Profitability (organization, product, and customer)
  - Peer group comparison
  - Productivity (efficiency, effectiveness)
- Risk Management

- Credit
- Interest
- Liquidity
- Foreign exchange
- Operating
- Capital adequacy

These are the main areas of focus for top management and the board. Each organizational unit reporting to the CEO and/or COO must provide relevant information to disclose the unit's status.

Look at each function (Figure 9) of an institution and list the manager's unique critical success factors (CSFs). CSFs are the things managers have to do right to succeed in their account-abilities. Also listed are corresponding information requirements, which indicate what must be in the reports to the managers on these functions.

These also can be translated into key performance indicators that must be reported to the CEO and COO.

Managers need basic information on budget and performance in spending and on staffing. They also need information on com-pliance to personnel policy and personnel management perform-ance in containing turnover, absenteeism, and building morale.

This is a summary view of what an institution needs. The thought here is to ensure that each key manager receives informa-tion and key performance indicators (KPIs) that will help him or her to manage better.

Information flowing to senior management must be relevant and action oriented. Therefore, in designing reports, question the usefulness and relevance of information.

An organizational hierarchy is pictured at the top of the next page.

All managers are responsible to COO (and CEO, board) for compliance, performance, and risk, and therefore, must provide information on these factors.

Reporting should be designed to serve the information needs of each management level. A high-level position such as the CEO

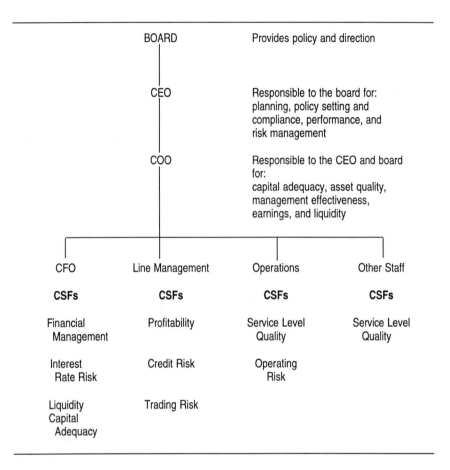

BOARD		Provides policy and direction	
CEO		Responsible to the board for: planning, policy setting and compliance, performance, and risk management	
COO		Responsible to the CEO and board for: capital adequacy, asset quality, management effectiveness, earnings, and liquidity	
CFO	Line Management	Operations	Other Staff
CSFs	**CSFs**	**CSFs**	**CSFs**
Financial Management	Profitability	Service Level Quality	Service Level Quality
Interest Rate Risk	Credit Risk	Operating Risk	
Liquidity Capital Adequacy	Trading Risk		

or COO usually requires a summary of information, but details must be easily available upon request. Also, a unified MIRS would provide information with increasing detail for each descending level.

Take the example of credit quality. This kind of information is the same at all levels but with more details as you descend in the organization's hierarchy. Let's follow the element of credit quality to see how it works, as follows:

Credit Quality

Level 1: Board, CEO, COO

Information—Loan quality, balances for each quality category.

Figure 9
Financial Institution Functions and Critical Success Factors

Function	Critical Success Factors (CSFs)	Information Requirements	Key Performance Indicators (KPIs)
Board CEO COO	Provide direction and leadership and manage the following:	Timely, accurate, and focused information	
	Planning		
	• Strategic	Strengths, weaknesses, opportunities, and threats	Objectives achievement
	• Budgeting	Budgets	Budget to actual performance
	• Policy	Areas needing policy	Compliance
	• Performance	Profitability by organization, product group, and major customer	Profitability ROA, ROE
		Productivity	Staffing levels Expense levels
	• Risk	Risk Management reporting on: Credit Interest rates Liquidity Trading Operations	Loan quality Interest sensitivity and gaps Asset/liability liquidity Net position Backlogs and errors
	Responsible for: Capital adequacy Asset quality Management effectiveness Earnings Liquidity	Early Warning	Exceptions
CFO	Timely, accurate, and focused reporting		Accuracy, timeliness, and focus

Figure 9 (Continued)

Function	Critical Success Factors (CSFs)	Information Requirements	Key Performance Indicators (KPIs)
	Financial Management		
	Financial accounting and compliance	Balance sheet,, income statement, regulatory reports	
	Planning	Planning and budgeting by organizational units	
	Cost Analysis	Unit costs, Fixed/variable capacity analysis	
	Profitability reporting	Organization, product and major customer	
	Financial Analysis	Costs/Benefits	
	Executive information reporting	Key Performance indicators	
	Tax planning and compliance	Laws and regulations	
	Asset/Liability management	Interest rates Balances Economic forecasts Cash flows	
LINE OFFICERS	Lending and portfolio management		
	Credit quality	Industry, geographic sector, and company factors	Loan ratings and policy compliance
	Revenue	P&L reports	Profitability
	Expense	Actual	Budget to actual
	Investment		
	Asset quality	Yields	Yields
	Revenue	Revenue	Revenue

Figure 9 (Continued)

Function	Critical Success Factors (CSFs)	Information Requirements	Key Performance Indicators (KPIs)
	Fiduciary		
	Deposit taking		
	Balances	Balances	Balances
	Cost	Cost of funds	Cost of funds
	Fee Income		
	Revenue	Revenue by organization, product, and customer	Revenue
	Trading		
	Profitability	Profit by trade and product	Profitability
	Trading risk	Positions	Policy compliance
Operations	Timeliness, efficiency, effectiveness	Response time, staffing levels to workload expenses, and volumes	Staff efficiency, objectives accomplished, and service level quality Response time Holdovers
Staff Organizations	Timely, accurate, and efficient support	Service requirements Bank objectives Expenses Volumes	Response time Accuracy Efficiency and cost
	Market awareness and identity	Market share	Marketing effectiveness

Level 2: Lending Group Head

Information—Loan quality, balances for each quality category. Balances by industry by quality.

Level 3: Lending Department Manager

Information—Loans, balances for each quality category. Balances by industry by quality.

Balances by major customer.

Balances by assigned account officer.

Obviously, there is much more to report on credit quality. Formats on credit quality reports on performance and risk management reporting are presented in Chapter 7. The idea here is to show how a unified MIRS will allow top management to procure more detailed information from the organizational hierarchy. Also shown is how a unified reporting system recedes from a detailed base to a high-level summary.

Conceptual and Functional Systems Design for Management Information Reporting

The previously mentioned information requirements suggest the support of a reporting system. Basically the general ledger and the applications systems provide raw data and information for the first level of management. The raw data and information are analyzed, condensed, and reformatted to produce management information reports. This processing sometimes requires human intervention. However, the ideal system is automated and requires no human intervention.

The following diagram shows how this process works:

	Primary Users			
	CFO	Line Management	Operations/EDP	Other Staff
Systems)	(1)	(3)	(5)	(2)
Used*)				
)	(2)	(4)		

* Systems:

(1) General Ledger

(2) Administrative: e.g., Payroll, Personnel

(3) Delivery: e.g., Loans, Deposits

(4) Customer: e.g., Customer Information File

(5) Transactions Processing

Basically five types of systems support financial institution management. They are (1) general ledger, (2) administrative, (3) delivery, (4) customer, and (5) transaction processing.

1. The general ledger (GL) supports financial accounting and management accounting. Sometimes it is difficult to get needed details out of your GL system.

2. The administrative systems such as payroll and the personnel system can support many users. For example, the personnel system could feed the general ledger as well as provide information to the personnel department.

3. The applications (delivery) systems include commercial loan system, consumer loan system, commercial deposit system, retail deposit system, and many others.

4. The customer system could be both wholesale and retail. Most institutions have a customer information file (CIF) on wholesale customers. Also, some financial institutions have created a CIF on retail customers.

5. Transaction processing systems such as check processing support operations and usually provide data rather than information. (Data are defined as unfocused information.)

What happens usually is that a system feeds raw data into an information resource module and its output is some form of management information. It isn't uncommon for a system to feed several modules or for one module to feed another. This process, diagrammed below, shows the commercial loan system feeding the customer information file (CIF) system. In turn, the CIF feeds the customer profitability reporting module.

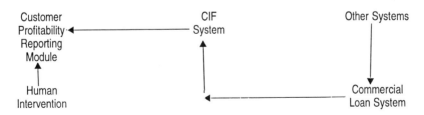

Static files that are poorly maintained can create problems.

Sometimes human intervention is needed even though one system may feed another system or module. Nevertheless, human intervention often slows the reporting of management information. When determining information requirements it is important to ascertain how much of it will be processed by a human versus computer.

Figure 10 shows basic systems, uses, and possible uses of the information gleaned from systems.

Human intervention increases the risk of error. However, full automation must be reconciled carefully—not accepted blindly.

What we have are various systems satisfying a number of information requirements throughout the organization, as follows:

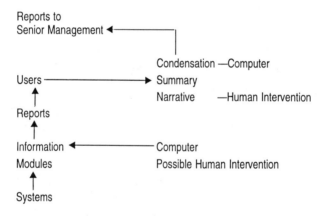

In this diagram, the systems feed information modules. The modules produce reports that are sent to users. Users process the information by condensing, summarizing, and providing interpretations. The condensed information is sent to top management in reports.

How to Design, Develop, and Implement a Management Information Reporting System

The driving force behind most management information reporting systems (MIRS) is a need for specific information. As mentioned

Figure 10
Basic Systems and Uses

Users	General Ledger	Administrative	Delivery	Customer	Transaction Processing
CFO	Financial Accounting (FA)	FA	FA		
	Mgmt. Accounting (MA)	MA Staff Administration	MA	MA	MA
Line Mgmt.	—	Staff Administration	Product Mgmt.	Customer Relationship Mgmt.	—
Operations/ EDP	—	Staff Administration	Production Mgmt.	Production Mgmt.	Production Mgmt.
Other Staff		Staff Administration			
Personnel (Human Resources)		Salary Administration Regulatory compliance			
Marketing			Market Segmentation Product Segmentation Product Mgmt.	Customer Segmentation	
Legal	Litigation support				
Audit	Auditing	Auditing	Auditing	Auditing	Auditing,
Strategic Planning	Planning Analysis	Planning Analysis	Planning Analysis	Planning Analysis	Planning Analysis

before, critical success factors play a significant role in determining the kinds of information to be reported. CSFs serve as a foundation for designing an MIRS.

Considerations vital in designing an MIRS are the kinds of information management needs to succeed in fulfilling its accountabilities. This information falls into several categories that include:

- Financial (revenue, expense, balances)
- Planning (strategic and operating budget)
- Personnel (staff levels)
- Compliance (regulatory, policy)

From these, management needs to know about variances, exceptions, and risks. They also use this information to measure performance.

Determine Information Needs

Once management's critical success factors and corresponding needs are determined you are ready to design management information reports. First, arrive at a consensus on what management will receive to clarify the information requirements. Sometimes requirements are changed when the potential recipients receive mock-ups of what the reports will look like. It helps to ask them to review the reports for usefulness of information being proposed and clarity of format. Then determine what information is available and define information gaps.

This step assesses information availability by matching information requirements against what is available and what is missing. Next, determine what resources are required to obtain this information. For example, additional staff and computer resources may be required along with systems modifications and report rewrites.

The cost of and time for modifying your information flow should be calculated. Management then can decide whether it is worthwhile to produce the extra information. Sometimes just a part of the additional information is costly. Management has to know specifically what is too costly to produce.

Management may ask that an MIRS be modified because of the timeliness of information. What is necessary here is a review of information flow to determine what the critical paths or dependencies are. Usually it is human intervention that causes delays. Another critical path would be dependency on another information system.

The following formula can be used for determining additional information needs:

Information required – Information available = Information gaps

Design Reports

A system map is needed to indicate what systems will be feeding the MIRS. The map also should show what data will be coming from the systems and when they will be available.

Necessary human intervention points, either in the feeder systems or the proposed MIRS, should be documented.

The system map should show how the MIRS process will flow from the beginning data to report distribution. To understand how the information will come together is essential. Necessary calculations should be noted. One of the most difficult tasks of building an MIRS is integrating information from several sources into a coherent system that provides timely and accurate reports.

Another problem that can develop in building an MIRS is having two sets of similar numbers floating around the institution. For example, loan department A may be reporting balances directly from the commercial loan system. Also, the MIRS may be reporting different loan balances for department A because of timing differences and management accounting adjustments. This problem will not disappear and must be solved by the person responsible for reporting and coordinating information. Reports should be labeled clearly as to source of information, purpose, and time.

Determine Impact of System Modifications

In building an MIRS, modifications probably will be needed in feeder systems to extract pertinent information. Some changes will be relatively easy, but others will require much time and expense. The cost of system modification should be weighed against the value of the information to be extracted from the feeder systems. That is, modifications must be worthwhile.

Conduct Feasibility Study

A feasibility study is needed to determine whether the project's cost will be offset by the value of the information produced. The following question needs to be asked: Is this a good time to be conducting such a project?

Write Detailed Specifications

A systems requirements and specifications document should be prepared to set forth what has to be done. It provides details on specific tasks. The level of detail should be agreed on before writing the document.

Flexibility to accommodate change is important. For example, banks frequently undergo organization change. A system should be able to accept change whether it be additions, deletions, or remapping of data.

Evaluate Software Packages

Are there any software packages available that will serve the needs specified? Software should be evaluated in terms of the system requirements.

Determine Present System Deficiencies

In addition to evaluating software packages your system should be evaluated against requirements, and deficiencies should be noted. An inquiry of what resources would be needed and the cost of modifications should be weighed. This can be compared with the cost of purchasing an outside software package.

Initiate Systems Modifications

It is important to construct a work plan showing what is to be done, by whom, and when. Also, what is deliverable should be mentioned. Figure 11 shows an example of a work plan.

In this sample work plan, task IA is identified in a brief description of what is to be done. The start-up and expected completion date and specifications are included. The anticipated starting date is the first day of "month 1." The expected completion date is the fifteenth day of "month 2." The task is expected to take 240 staff hours. Therefore, Evans, the assigned staff person, will have to work full-time on the chore. No dependencies exist in the sample. That is, the task requires no preliminary work. What is expected of the task can be delivered. The reference made to specification IA comes from the systems requirements and specifications document.

Test Systems Modifications

In this phase, systems modifications are tested and corrections or changes are made. It is important to stay with the original specifications and work plan as much as possible. Sometimes issues will surface that require a reevaluation of the original specifications and work plan. Such changes need to be reviewed carefully for their effect on specific areas and the overall project. Don't jeopardize the success of a project by making too many changes half way through it. Also, be reasonable with the speed of the project. Haste and excessive changes can cause costly errors.

Implement Systems

In this phase, the MIRS is activated and actual reports are produced. If the testing was done properly, few glitches will appear.

However, these first reports should be reviewed carefully for accuracy before they are distributed. Credibility of information is at stake. Once reports are in their hands, the recipients will evaluate the MIRS based on first impressions. Thus, it is important that the data are good.

Running the MIRS in tandem with whatever existed before is prudent until all needed corrections and modifications are made.

Post-Implementation Review

There is no doubt that parts of the MIRS will need debugging or changes. In the post-implementation review, the system's output is evaluated against the original objectives. Changes are flagged and evaluated for possible system modifications.

Figure 11
Example of a Work Plan

Task	Month 1	Month 2	Staff Hours	Assigned Staff Person	Dependencies	Deliverable	Hours to Date[1]
IA—Program Commercial Loan System includes branch location and industry codes for each loan.	S——1st	T——15th	240	Evans	None	Program modification that includes location and industry codes for each loan. By branch booked and by industry. (See specification 1A.)	

S = Start.
T = Target.
C = Completion.

[1] For project monitoring.

Document Procedures

Once system modifications and implementation issues are resolved, procedures are documented for those who will use the
system's output. The procedures provide a systems map. Processing and calculation sequences are detailed and algorithms and for-
mulas are provided. Also, feeder-system inputs and details on
how the system will function are specified.

Summary

This chapter presented an overview of what to consider when developing a management information reporting system (MIRS). The
information is directed at the executive who will be asking others
to develop an MIRS.

Developing an MIRS can be expensive and time consuming.
This is why it is important to determine its purpose. Then the
needs of those who will receive reports can be articulated. The
MIRS objective should be to help individuals manage their accountabilities more effectively. This is done by providing them
with clear, focused, relevant, and timely information.

5

Cost and Profitability Reporting

Cost and profitability reporting (C&PR) is central to many management decisions. To accommodate decision making, financial institutions need a good C&PR system. The process begins by reviewing what your institution has against what it needs and identifying information gaps. You then design, develop, and implement a system that will fill information needs. They are usually defined by identifying the uses of the information. For example, cost information can be used in setting prices.

The overall process of identifying needs and building a system can be expensive. Many factors must be considered. Each path has its cost but sometimes an institution has several options. Which is best for the institution may be difficult to decide. However, through careful analysis an informed decision can be made.

This chapter covers some of the critical issues to resolve in building or revamping a cost and profitability reporting system. A checklist is included.

An overall design of a basic system is presented in this chapter, providing a comprehensive and integrated view of how a system should work.

This chapter also will give the reader basic tools that will help determine management's needs and how to design, develop, and implement a system.

Determining Management's Information Needs

Before designing a system, it is critical to find out what is needed for decision making. This can be accomplished through interviews with key persons and making surveys. Brief interviews that are structured can be worthwhile. They can be conducted with a combination of yes/no and open-ended questions.

To get people to say what they want and need is usually difficult. They may know intuitively what they want. Nonetheless, it is the management accountant's job to bring these data to the surface. Your questioning can be a guide toward an agenda and thereby surface their needs.

When written survey forms are given to senior management, results are mixed. Some won't fill them out, others will scoff at them, and some will cooperate fully. Forms should be brief and concise and never consume several hours of a manager's time. Therefore, most managers probably won't respond to a 14-page questionnaire that requires fill-in paragraphs, yes/no answers, and multiple choice questions.

The goal is to discover management's information needs. This means sorting out what is needed for decision making versus what is nice to have. This is possible by probing what the requested information is intended for. For example, a reply may be that unit-cost information is needed for pricing products. You are then in a position to probe further on how a manager wants these data presented.

Once management's needs and the intended use of the information is determined, you can check what information is available. The difference is the information gap that must be filled. By going through this process, you will be able to design intelligently a cost and profitability reporting system.

What Is Cost and Profitability Reporting?

Costing information provides the basis for profitability reporting and provides data on product costs, overhead, and transfer pricing. All go into profitability reports. Cost analysis data are compiled to report accurately relationships of work effort and expense toward building something of value or worth.

Cost data can be reported by showing how the elements of a unit-cost build up. This can be reported in several ways and show the cost of each function building to a product. Or it can show a build-up of unit time multiplied by an hourly expense rate, as in standard costing. Still another way is to show the build-up of line-item expenses, such as compensation and other operating expenses, and divide them by a volume count. This is done in average item costing. Costing reports usually provide an audit trail of how expenses were applied to a cost object.

Profitability reports reflect cost data in several ways. Its use depends on the profitability report being produced. Basically, three dimensions are defined in profitability reporting: organization, product, and customer. Organization profitability is usually the easiest to produce. If it reports indirects, management accounting intervention is necessary. Therefore, allocations are part of this reporting process, especially if it only measures direct income and expense. Following this complexity is product profitability reporting. In the progression of complexity, customer profitability reporting is the highest. To produce customer profitability reports, unit costs must be known. Also, many allocations have to be performed.

A profitability triad diagram appears as follows:

Organization	Product	Customer
Profitability	Profitability	Profitability
Reporting	Reporting	Reporting

Cost Allocation Systems

The diagram shows only one way that it could work. Some institutions have their reporting on a sequential progression, beginning with their cost-allocation system feeding organization reporting; then organization feeding product, and then product feeding customer. There are many variations to this. However, product and customer profitability, particularly, depend on unit-cost data.

What to Resolve in Building an Integrated Cost and Profitability Reporting System

At the top of the list of issues to resolve are (1) how the output is going to be used, (2) who will receive it, and (3) what is available from feeder systems. These and many other important issues have to be resolved before building a system. Management philosophy will influence many of the factors. Therefore, flexibility should be built into the system to accommodate today's philosophy and what it might be tomorrow.

Seven basic areas must be reviewed in building a system. They are: the institution's business orientation, intended use of current information, reporting strengths and weaknesses, information requirements, information availability, management accounting issues, and systems issues and solutions.

The Financial Institution's Business Orientation

The financial institution's organization structure and market focus should be clarified. Organization types include unit institution, branch institution, and a confederation of quasi-independent institutions (acquired institutions). Emphasis on such things as wholesale versus retail and domestic versus international is important in specifying information requirements. The institution's market orientation also should be considered. For example, if it is primarily an agricultural lending institution its requirements will differ from an institution that has a diversified market orientation.

The Intended Use of Information

Decision making and management control are the most common reasons for information being sent to management. Management style often dictates the format, level of detail, and kinds of information to be reported.

Management decisions are numerous. Therefore, the analyst must focus on those accountabilities, and, hence, decisions that affect the institution most, and provide management with the right information. "Need to know" information obviously should have priority over "nice to have" information.

Current Reporting Strengths and Weaknesses

Most managers can readily tell the weaknesses of a reporting system. Common weaknesses include late delivery, too much data, lack of focus, inaccuracies, inequitable allocations, unexplainable methodology, and nonavailability of pertinent information. Each of these should be analyzed specifically and possible solutions should be proposed.

A common need is to assess the sophistication of the institution's reporting: How comprehensive and complex is it?

The following are areas to assess:

- Cost analysis
- Organization profitability reporting
- Product profitability reporting
- Customer profitability reporting
- Profit planning and reporting

Information Requirements

Brief interviews with management personnel will help to determine information requirements. Timing and frequency of availability must be considered when determining requirements.

Preciseness is needed on reporting needs for the following information:

- Revenue
- Expenses
- Volumes
- Balances
- Unit costs
- Allocations
- Transfers

Additionally, report formats should be specified. This may require several revisions before a specific format is accepted.

Information Availability

Once the information requirements have been agreed to, then determine what is available. Also, the amount of human and machine intervention necessary to produce the information should be measured. An overall functional systems map should be drawn to show the information flow.

Information gaps will appear, this being the difference between what is available and what is required. Solutions on how to obtain such information or adjustments to the requirements are needed before the overall reporting design is final.

Management Accounting Issues

Several management accounting issues have to be resolved in building a profitability-reporting system. These issues include, but are not limited to, the following:

- Funds transfer pricing methodology.
- Costing methodology (standard versus nonstandard).
- Expense variance recovery.
- Shadow reporting (dual reporting, memo and double counting; and fee, expense, and balance splitting).
- Loan loss charging and reserve assignment.
- Equity allocation.

Each issue is covered in later chapters.

Systems Issues and Solutions

Solutions to systems issues range from simple to complex and some can be costly. Much thought and analysis must be done in costly situations to determine the dollar value of providing information. Also, there are times when an expensive alternative appears to be the only one, but further analysis and discussion may turn up a more cost-effective possibility. Some of the issues in systems information resource management include:

- Availability of data, such as volume counts, balances, fee revenue.

- Linkages and feeds, from one system or process to another.
- Timeliness of information availability.
- Mainframe versus microcomputer applications.
- Systems staff availability.
- Systems capacity.
- Technological obsolescence.
- Cost of building a system.
- Cost of maintaining a system.

There are other systems issues to resolve, but the main idea is to give careful thought to all relevant issues in planning the project.

Conceptual Cost and Profitability Reporting System Design

The ideal cost-and-profitability functional system is one where: (1) cost data is compiled and routed with limited difficulty, and (2) where organization, product, and customer profitability tie into or reconcile with one another and the general ledger. For many institutions, this isn't easy to achieve because of systems constraints. Also, management accounting technology expertise varies from institution to institution. Therefore, two important constraints are system limitations and personnel expertise.

As stated previously, organization profitability reporting is the least complex of the profitability triad. This is followed by product profitability reporting, and lastly customer profitability reporting (medium to large corporate customers). See Figures 12, 13, and 14. Figure 12 shows the profitability triad. Figure 13 provides a complexity scale of profitability reporting. Figure 14 is a grid of what is required and the reporting uses of each triad member.

Figure 15 provides a look at a basic functional system design. It shows how a cost system interfaces with profitability reporting

Figure 12
Profitability Triad

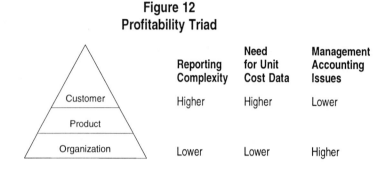

	Reporting Complexity	Need for Unit Cost Data	Management Accounting Issues
Customer	Higher	Higher	Lower
Organization	Lower	Lower	Higher

and how a host of management accounting issues are relevant to the system.

Cost and Profitability Reporting: Functional System Design

1. *Feeder Systems*
    The feeder systems management accounting uses include administrative, general ledger, and delivery systems. These feeder systems provide the following data: revenue, expense, and volume (including balances). Depending on the source and application, the data may be available from organization, product line, or customer. The feeder systems provide data to management accounting.

Figure 13
Three Dimensions of Profitability

	Organization	Product	Customer	Total Institution
Revenue	$100	$100	$100	$100
Expense/Costs	$ 75	$ 75	$ 75	$ 75
Profitability	$ 25	$ 25	$ 25	$ 25

Figure 14
Report Requirements and Uses

Report	Information Requirements	Optional	Possible Uses of Information Measurement		Decisions	
			Performance	Profit	Pricing	Other*
Customer (Wholesale)	Unit cost data, revenue, balances (loans and deposits), expenses, funds charge and credit, volumes, billing, sic codes, total relationship information	Compensating balance verification mechanism tied to specific product usage. Market segmentation	X	X	X	X
Product	Unit cost data, revenue, balances (if applicable), expenses, funds charge and credit, and volumes		X	X	X	X
Organization	Revenue, balances (if applicable), expenses (direct, transfers, and allocations), funds charge and credit, and volumes		X	X		X

* Other.
Initiate, continue, exit

Figure 15
Cost and Profitability Reporting

Functional System Design

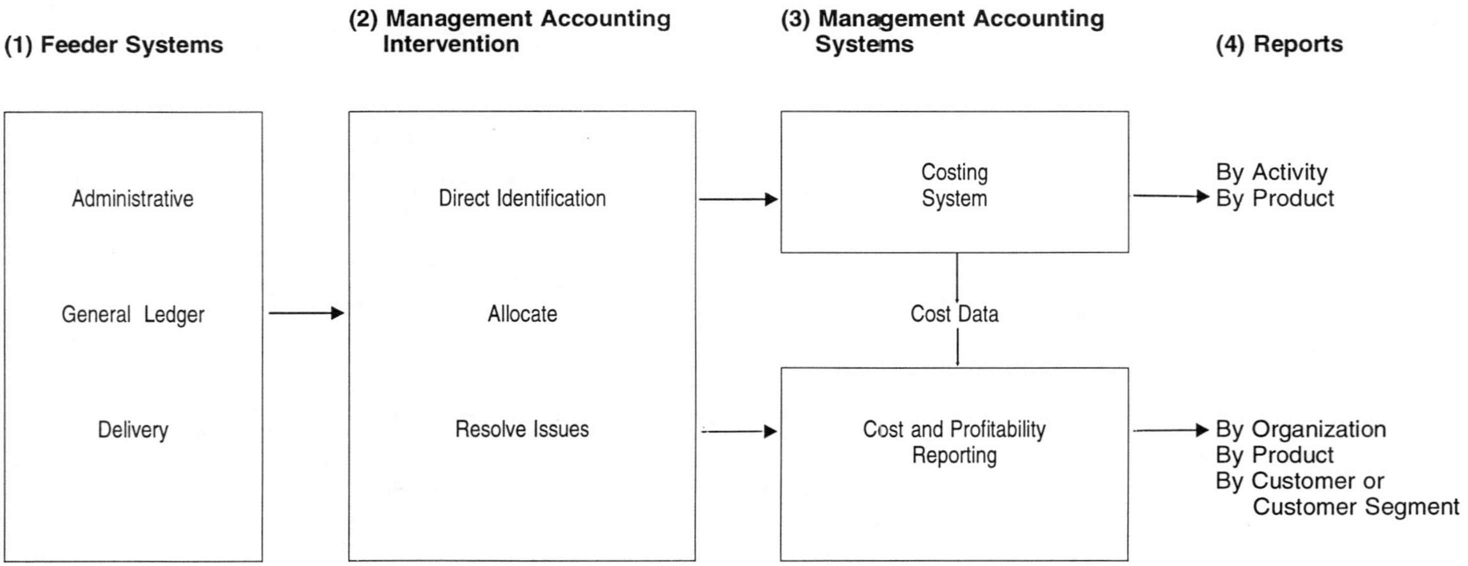

(1) Feeder Systems

(2) Management Accounting Intervention

(3) Management Accounting Systems

(4) Reports

Administrative

General Ledger

Delivery

Direct Identification

Allocate

Resolve Issues

Costing System

Cost Data

Cost and Profitability Reporting

By Activity
By Product

By Organization
By Product
By Customer or
   Customer Segment

2. *Management Accounting Intervention*
   Management accounting ensures that the direct capturing is applied to the proper reporting object. It verifies the integrity of the numbers and decides subjectively how to allocate indirect items. This involves selecting an equitable and relevant basis and developing a corresponding algorithm.

3. *Management Accounting (MA) Systems*
   The two most common MA systems for profitability reporting are a costing system and a cost-and-profitability reporting system. A costing system collects expense and volume data and routes it to a cost object such as an activity or product. The system usually collects and reports the data as a unit cost for each cost object being reported. A cost and profitability reporting system uses data from the costing system and aligns costs with revenue and reports profitability.

Designing Cost Analysis Reports

The first step in designing cost analysis reports involves three questions: What is their intended use? How often will they be used? Who will receive them?

- **What is their intended use?**

As mentioned earlier, cost analysis data has many uses. It can be used to (1) support pricing decisions, (2) provide cost recovery and control information, and (3) determine profitability reporting. Each of these has its unique importance. For sample reports, refer to Figures 16, 17, and 18.

In Cost Report 1: When cost data is used to support pricing information, it usually is formatted as a product cost. To do this, you must develop unit costs that coincide with a product. A good way to do this for fee-based products is to develop unit costs for each product listed in your institution's schedule of fees and charges. This way decision makers will know the profit impact of their product-pricing decisions. A cost report that supports prod-

Figure 16
Cost Report 1

Product Group—Depository Products
Product Line—Consumer DDA

Products	Per Debit	Per Account Monthly Maintenance	Open an Account	Close an Account	Average Balance	Average Monthly Cost of Funds	Volume		
							Per Month Debits	Number of Accounts	
Discount Account	$0.21	$ 5.37	$15.87	$ 8.10	$ 158	0	8	1,850	
Regular Account	0.21	7.29	16.24	8.52	689	0	35	3,725	
Executive Account	0.21	13.53	23.48	11.43	1,775	7.77	4	2,028	

Cost Data for Pricing Decisions

Figure 17
Cost Report 2

Service Center Recovery Report
Current Month Over/(Under) Budget
Favorable (F)/Unfavorable (U)

Variance Analysis

Activity	Actual Unit Cost	Volume	Total Costs	Recovery Amount/Percent		Variance Due to Volume	Variance Due to Spending and Efficiency
				(1)		(2)	(3)
Process a							
Debit	$0.16	7,603	$1,216	1,140	91.1	($16)	76 U

Calculations

(1) Planned Cost = Price
$.15 x 7,603 = $1,140.45
Recovery

(2) Planned Volume   7,702
less Actual Volume   −7,603
Variance (under)   (99)
X $0.16 Actual Cost
=   ($16)

(3) Planned Cost $ 0.15
less Actual Cost   −0.16
Variance $−0.01 U
X   7,603 Actual Volume
= $76 U

Figure 18
Cost Report 3

Current Month
Product Group—Depository Products
Product Line—Consumer DDA
Product—Discount Account—Monthly Maintenance

Activity	Per Month Expense	Per Month Volume	Activity Unit Cost	Product Volume	Frequencied (Product Aligned) Unit Cost
Deposits					
Compensation	$1,184				
Other Operating	395				
Data Processing	844				
Total	2,423	5,550	$0.436	1,850	$1.31 ($2,423 ÷ 1,850 = $1.31)
Statements					
Compensation	651				
Other Operating	253				
Data Processing	1,482				
Total	2,386	1,850	1.290	1,850	1.29
Inquiries					
Compensation	942				
Other Operating	153				
Data Processing	107				
Total	1,202	582	2.070	1,850	0.65 ($1,202 ÷ 1,850 = $0.65)
Branch Administration			1.420		1.42
General and Administrative			0.700		0.70
Total Product					$5.37

Cost Data Used for Profitability Reporting

uct pricing will show how volumes and unit costs build up. It should separate direct from indirect costs.

In Cost Report 2: Cost data that provide cost recovery and control information usually are designed for use by cost analysts and the service center manager. The recovery reporting aspect may be referred to as "transfer out effectiveness." It provides a check of how well the transfer rates are performing against actual expenses. Sometimes further clarity is provided by reporting variances attributable to volume variances, spending variances, and efficiency variances.

In Cost Report 3: Cost reports used for profitability reporting can be similar in content to reports used in pricing. However, cost reports may contain trend information and budget to actual comparisons. Product profitability reporting can be reported on a stand-alone-product basis or by product within an organization. Cost data for this reporting would be derived from the basic product cost report mentioned in this section.

- **How often will they be used?**

Determining frequency is important because it sets the requirements for how often data are to be extracted, calculated, and reported. Ask: "How often is the report really needed?"

- **Who is to receive the cost reports?**

It is prudent to prepare a proposed distribution list before developing a report. This is a test of its necessity. Find out who needs the report and what they will do with it. This provides an opportunity to review proposed formats with those to whom you will be sending the report.

Cost Report 1, which supports pricing decisions, should go to product management and/or marketing. If your institution has a pricing committee, it could also be included on the distribution list.

Cost Report 2, which involves cost recovery and control, should be sent to service center managers, cost analysts, and the controller and/or manager of cost analysis and control.

Cost Report 3 is used for profitability reporting. It is similar to Cost Report 1, but its routes and reports accommodate profitability reporting from different format perspectives. For example, Cost

Report 3 allows an institution to present cost data by product by organization, by product by activity, and by product by expense category.

Next, look at possible cost report formats. Cost information on pricing decisions can be reported by product. Usually a pricing committee wants to review several products in a product line at one time, therefore, they may be listed in this report.

The variations and possibilities for report content and format are immense. They depend on the institution's costing system's architecture. How the data are accumulated and routed will determine largely the cost report content and format possibilities.

Menu of Data Requirements for Designing a Cost and Profitability Reporting System

There are several data requirement issues to resolve in selecting a vendor system or designing one's own cost-accounting system. The following checklist of possible data requirements may be considered as you proceed with designing cost and profitability reporting systems. (An x indicates relevant system consideration.)

Checklist of Possible Data Requirements

	System	Profitability Reporting		
Menu Feature	Costing	Organization	Product	Customer
	C	O	P	C
1. Cost Allocations				
Responsibility Center (RC) to RC	x	x		
RC to Profit Centers Only	x	x		
RC to Products Only	x	x	x	
Sequential Close Out	x	x		
Simultaneous Close Out	x	x		
Bases				
User Defined	x	x		

Checklist of Possible Data Requirements (Continued)

	C	O	P	C
Bases (Continued)				
Specified and Fixed	x	x		
Range and Scope				
Number of RCs (Allocators and Allocatees)	x	x		
Number of Products	x	x	x	
Overhead	x	x	x	x
Automated Mechanism	x	x	x	x
Human Intervention Required	x	x	x	x
2. Time Frame				
Historical Data				
Plan	x	x	x	x
Actual	x	x	x	x
Current Data				
Plan	x	x	x	x
Actual	x	x	x	x
Planned				
Future	x	x	x	x
Forecast	x	x	x	x
Automated Mechanism	x	x	x	x
Human Intervention Required	x	x	x	x
3. Costing Parameters				
Average Item Costing	x			
Standard Costing	x			
Relative Values	x			
Work Measurement				
Tasks	x			
Activities	x			
Time Ladders	x			
Unit costs	x	x	x	x
Number of Unit Costs	x	x	x	x
Number of Activities	x	x	x	
Number of Products	x	x	x	x

Checklist of Possible Data Requirements (Continued)

	C	O	P	C
Fixed/Variable	X	X	X	
Number of Cost Pools	X		X	
Calculates Activity Costs	X			
Calculates Product Costs	X			
Automated System	X			
Human Intervention Required	X			
4. Cost Transfers				
Expense Line Items	X	X	X	X
Activity Costs	X	X	X	
Product Costs	X	X	X	X
Automated Transfer Mechanism	X	X	X	X
Number of Activities	X	X		
Number of Products	X	X	X	X
Number of RCs	X	X	X	
Automated Mechanism	X	X	X	
Human Intervention Required	X	X	X	
5. Reports				
To/From Allocations	X	X		
Activity Routing Trail (Cost Buildup)	X	X	X	
Product Routing Trail (Cost Buildup)	X	X	X	
To/From Transfers	X	X	X	
Variances				
Time Period to Time Period	X	X	X	X
Plan to Actual	X	X	X	
Expense Volume, Activity	X	X	X	
Spending (Expense)	X	X	X	
Efficiency	X	X	X	
Revenue		X	X	X
Balances		X	X	X
Report Writer Flexibility, (User Specified) (Format and Content)	X	X	X	X

Checklist of Possible Data Requirements (Continued)

	C	O	P	C
Hierarchy (Roll-up from Bottom to Top)	x	x	x	x
Reports by Line Item (Revenue, Expense, Balance, Volume, Activity Categories)		x	x	x
Report by Product	x	x	x	
Report by RC	x	x	x	
Wholesale/Commercial	x	x	x	x
Retail	x	x	x	x
Total Customer Relationship				x
Asset-Based (e.g., Loans)				x
Liability-Based (e.g., Deposits)				x
Fee-based Services (e.g., Cash Management)				x
Automated System	x	x	x	x
Human Intervention Required	x	x	x	x

Customer Grouping

	C	O	P	C
By Product				x
By SIC (Industry)				x
By Geography				x
By Account Officer				x
By Organization				x
By Deposit Size				x
By Asset Size				x
By Loan Amount				x
By Credit Rating				x
By Their Revenue				x
By Institution's Revenue				x

6. Flexibility

	C	O	P	C
Top Down Changes	x	x	x	
Bottom-Up Changes	x	x	x	
Sensitivity Analyses (what-if gaming)	x	x	x	x
Adjustments				
Positive	x	x	x	x

Checklist of Possible Data Requirements (Continued)

	C	O	P	C
Adjustments (Continued)				
Negative	x	x	x	x
7. Storage				
Volume, Activity	x	x	x	x
Balances	x	x	x	x
Revenue	x	x	x	x
Expenses	x	x	x	x
Cost Data	x	x	x	x
Determine How Many Months	x	x	x	x
Determine How Much Data	x	x	x	x
8. Download Capability				
From Delivery Systems	x	x	x	x
From Administrative Systems	x	x	x	x
From General Ledger	x	x	x	x
From Other Modules	x	x	x	x
Automated Mechanism	x	x	x	x
Human Intervention Required	x	x	x	x
9. Upload Capability				
To Mainframe Systems	x	x	x	x
To Minicomputer Systems	x	x	x	x
To Microcomputer Systems and Modules	x	x	x	x
Automated Mechanism	x	x	x	x
Human Intervention Required	x	x	x	x
10. Integrity				
Tie to General Ledger (GL)	x	x	x	x
Forced Balance Exception Reporting	x	x	x	x
Reconcile to GL	x	x	x	x
Automated Mechanism	x	x	x	x
Human Intervention Required	x	x	x	x

Checklist of Possible Data Requirements (Continued)

	C	O	P	C
11. Information Availability				
From GL Revenue, Expenses, Balances	x	x	x	x
From Administrative Expenses, Staff Count	x	x	x	x
From Delivery Balance, Volume, Revenue, and Expense	x	x	x	x
Automated Extract	x	x	x	x
Human Intervention Required	x	x	x	x
12. Other Data Requirements				
Number of Customers				x
Waived Fee Tracking		x	x	x
Analysis Charges Tracking		x	x	x
Compensating Balances				x
Customer Billing				x
13. Management Accounting Issues				
• Funds Transfer Pricing (FTP)		x	x	
Single Pool				
Internal Rates				
Market Rates				
Multiple Pool				
Internal Rates				
Market Rates				
Number of Pools				
Matched Funding				
Internal Rates				
Market Rates				
Number of Pools				
Money Desk Concept				
Contract Spreads				

Checklist of Possible Data Requirements (Continued)

	C	O	P	C
Pricing Structure				
Money Desk Concept				
All				
Automated				
Mechanism and Tracking				
Early Payoffs and Tracking				
Human Intervention Required				
• Customer Funds Pricing				X
Deposit Funds Analysis Charges				
Automated Mechanism and Tracking				
Human Intervention Required				
• Equity Allocation	X	X	X	X
• Notational Reporting	X	X	X	X
• Cost of Carry				
Nonearning Assets		X	X	X
Nonperforming Loans		X	X	X
• Allocation of Loan Loss Reserves and Write-offs		X	X	X

The Cost Study Process—Average Item Costing (AIC) Methodology

One of several alternatives of how to develop costs is average item costing. However, it represents a basic common approach. Figure 19 provides an example of how AIC works. It is a high-level overview, but from it one can understand the essence of the process. Average item costing methodology in this example involves nine basic steps. They are (1) conduct preliminary activities, (2) gather information, (3) review information, (4) identify, assign, and allocate expenses to responsibility centers (RCs), (5) identify, assign, and allocate RC expenses to revenue producing functions, (6) identify products, volumes, and relative values, (7) allocate functional expenses to products, (8) calculate product unit costs, and (9) disseminate information—write report.

1. *Conducting preliminary activities.* Determine purpose of cost study and intended uses. Communicate project needs and requirements to concerned parties such as senior management.

2. *Gather information.* Obtain organization chart and expense data. Determine necessary exclusions or additions. Determine bases from expense allocations.

3. *Review information.* Review researched information with appropriate management and staff. Obtain agreement with them and respond to suggested modifications.

4. *Identify, assign, and allocate expenses to responsibility centers (RCs).* This step is not necessary for institutions that already have RC reporting that also allocates indirect expenses.

   In Figure 19, staff compensation is directly identifiable to RCs. However, the $3 in "other operating" expenses must be allocated. The basis selected is each RC's percentage of compensation to the total compensation.

5. *Identify, assign, and allocate RC expenses to revenue producing functions.* In the example, there is only one revenue-producing function—paying and receiving. Therefore, it received all of the expenses.

6. *Identify products, volumes, and relative values.* In the example, paying and receiving has two products—payments and receipts. Product volumes are to be identified. Also, relative values are developed. Usually this is done by observation and interviews with key persons. For a detailed explanation of relative values refer to *Cost Accounting for Financial Institutions* (Leonard Cole, Probus, 1994).

7. *Allocate functional expenses to products.* The expenses for paying and receiving are allocated to the two products based on each product's relative value. The relative val-

Figure 19
Cost Study Process Diagram (Overview)
Average Item Costing (AIC) Methodology

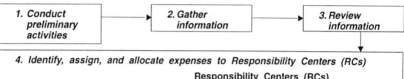

1. Conduct preliminary activities	→	2. Gather information	→	3. Review information

4. Identify, assign, and allocate expenses to Responsibility Centers (RCs)

		Responsibility Centers (RCs)		
Expenses	Total	D.P.	Paying & Receiving	Basis
Compensation	$6	$2	$4	Direct
Other Operating	3	1	2	Comp. %
Total	$9	$3	$6	

5. Identify, assign, and allocate RC expenses to revenue-producing functions

Responsibility		Function(s)	
Centers	Total	Paying & Receiving	Other
D.P.	$3	$3	$0
Paying & Receiving	6	6	0
	$9	$9	$0

6. Identify products, volumes, and develop relative values

Products	Volume	Relative Values
Payments	100	2
Receipts	200	1

7. Allocate functional expenses to products

Function	Total Expenses	Products Payments	Receipts	Cost Distribution Basis
Paying & Receiving	$9	$4.50	$4.50	Relative Values

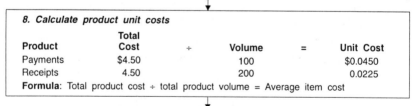

```
100 x 2 = 200      200 ÷ 400 = 50%
200 x 1 = 200      .5 x $9 = $4.50
Total    400
```

8. Calculate product unit costs

Product	Total Cost	÷	Volume	=	Unit Cost
Payments	$4.50		100		$0.0450
Receipts	4.50		200		0.0225

Formula: Total product cost ÷ total product volume = Average item cost

9. Disseminate information: write report

ues are applied against volumes. Then a percentage to total is calculated for each product's relative value.

8. *Calculate product unit costs.* The total cost for each product is divided by its volume to arrive at a product unit cost.

9. *Disseminate information and write the report.* A report is written that explains the methodology and uses of the cost data.

The Cost Study Process—Standard Costing

There are several alternatives for developing standard unit costs. However, the example in Figure 20 represents a basic common approach. It is high level but provides nine basic steps to standard costing. They are (1) conduct preliminary activities, (2) gather information, (3) review information, (4) identify, assign, and allocate expenses to responsibility centers (RCs), (5) identify, assign, and allocate RC expenses to revenue-producing functions, (6) identify products and volumes and develop time standards, (7) develop hourly expense rates for each function or processing center, (8) calculate product unit costs, and (9) disseminate information— write report.

The differences between AIC and standard costing include:

- Step 6—Time standards are developed in lieu of defining relative values.

- Step 7—Hourly expense rates are developed for processing centers in lieu of allocating expenses to products.

- Step 8—Product unit costs are calculated using time standards in lieu of dividing total costs by total volume.

Standard and Nonstandard Costing—
Comparative Impact and Issues

Standard Costing

Standard costing methodology is best used in processing areas where the work is repetitive and predictable. It allows management the ability to sort and quantify the economic impact of vol-

Figure 20
Cost Study Process Diagram (Overview)
Standard Costing Methodology

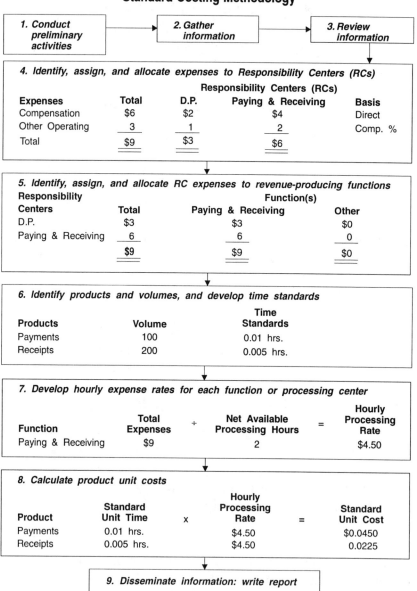

1. Conduct preliminary activities → **2. Gather information** → **3. Review information**

4. Identify, assign, and allocate expenses to Responsibility Centers (RCs)

Expenses	Total	D.P.	Paying & Receiving	Basis
			Responsibility Centers (RCs)	
Compensation	$6	$2	$4	Direct
Other Operating	3	1	2	Comp. %
Total	$9	$3	$6	

5. Identify, assign, and allocate RC expenses to revenue-producing functions

Responsibility Centers	Total	Paying & Receiving	Other
		Function(s)	
D.P.	$3	$3	$0
Paying & Receiving	6	6	0
	$9	$9	$0

6. Identify products and volumes, and develop time standards

Products	Volume	Time Standards
Payments	100	0.01 hrs.
Receipts	200	0.005 hrs.

7. Develop hourly expense rates for each function or processing center

Function	Total Expenses	÷	Net Available Processing Hours	=	Hourly Processing Rate
Paying & Receiving	$9		2		$4.50

8. Calculate product unit costs

Product	Standard Unit Time	x	Hourly Processing Rate	=	Standard Unit Cost
Payments	0.01 hrs.		$4.50		$0.0450
Receipts	0.005 hrs.		$4.50		0.0225

9. Disseminate information: write report

ume, spending, and efficiency variances. Standard costs are prescriptive. That is, they prescribe the cost, the time standards, and hourly processing rate. Standard costs provide a benchmark for management to compare actual occurrences.

A standard costing structure and system can be costly to develop and maintain. A large data base is needed. A relatively large staff also is needed to maintain the standards.

Nonstandard Costing (Average Item, Actual)

A nonstandard system can be relatively easy to develop and maintain. Actual costs are known. Methodology and data flows tend to be simple. The cost to develop and maintain a nonstandard system can be minimal when compared to a standard system.

Nonstandard costs are volume and spending sensitive. Therefore, they will fluctuate with volume and expense changes. Inefficiencies of processing centers using this method are not readily visible to management. Excess capacity may be difficult to discern.

Information Maintenance Requirements for a Cost and Profitability Reporting System

Regardless of the complexity of a system, a considerable amount of information has to be maintained. The degree of maintenance depends largely on the following factors:

- Degree of automation.
- Costing methodology employed, standard versus AIC.
- Frequency of scheduled information updates.

Degree of Automation. In an automated system, data usually are updated and reported monthly. In a manual or semiautomated system, data may be updated and reported at wider intervals. For example: unit costs are reported annually and product profitability, monthly.

Costing Methodology Employed. A standard costing system is considerably more complex and time consuming to maintain than average item costing (AIC). It isn't desirable for an institution using standard costing to have several hundred time standards. Therefore, a relatively large staff is required to maintain the standards. Reorganizations and work-flow changes can render a standard or group of standards obsolete.

Operational Aspects. A typical management accounting cost and profitability reporting, includes the following:

- Frequency of scheduled information updates. Some financial institutions update their unit costs monthly. Others update their unit costs annually. The interval of updates depends on management philosophy and policy. Generally, the more frequent updates require more resources.

- Download or extraction from administrative, delivery, and general ledger systems—usually monthly.

- Alignment of revenue, expense, balance, and volume data to activities, products, organizations, and customers.

- Development of unit cost.

- Alignment of unit-cost data to organizations, products, and customers.

- Allocation of overhead.

- Frequency analysis. Adjusting for volume differences when combining tasks or activities.

- Calculation and analysis of variances, e.g., budget to actual.

- Verification of tie or reconcilement to institution's general ledger.

- Production reports.

It is important to note that a costing system serves as a foundation for product and customer profitability reporting.

Figure 21 at the end of this chapter is a matrix that serves as an indicator of what is usually maintained in a cost and profitability reporting system. To achieve preciseness, the following breakouts are presented: costing, organizational profitability reporting, product profitability reporting, and customer profitability reporting.

Summary

Designing, developing, implementing, and maintaining a cost and profitability reporting system involves many factors.

Designing the system requires that you know the intended uses for the information. It also necessitates knowing what kind of information or data are available to feed the system. However, be cautious not to design a system that is overly complex and costly to build and maintain. The main goal should be to attain a comfortable level of accuracy in a cost effective manner.

Developing the system involves evaluating existing software, making in-house system changes, defining data to be input in the system, researching the data, aligning the data, and building the system.

Implementing the system entails bringing the data into the system and creating useful reports. Maintaining the system is a continuing process. The effort required depends on how frequently information must be updated and the method used.

Two basic considerations in building a cost and profitability reporting system are the institution's management philosophy and the need for flexibility to accommodate change.

Figure 21
Information to Be Maintained in a Cost and Profitability Reporting System

Legend—T = Typical Requirement; P = Possible Requirement; H = High; M = Medium; L = Low.

Specific Information to Be Maintained	Costing	Organizational Profitability	Product Profitability	Customer Profitability	Ongoing Maintenance Require-ments	Comments
Mapping of tasks, activities, and products within a responsibility center (RC)	T				H	Initial identification and ongoing maintenance are high. Frequent changes in organizations and processing (work flow) are not unusual.
Relative values of tasks, activities, and products within an RC (if relative values are used)	T				H	Initial identification could be high. Ongoing maintenance requires reevaluating relative value mix.
Time standards of tasks, activities, and products within an RC (if time standards are used)	T				H	Initial development and ongoing maintenance are very high. Not unusual for a typical standard costing system to have several hundred standards to develop and maintain. Huge data storage requirement.

Figure 21 (Continued)

Legend—T = Typical Requirement; P = Possible Requirement; H = High; M = Medium; L = Low.

Specific Information to Be Maintained	Costing	Organizational Profitability	Product Profitability	Customer Profitability	Ongoing Maintenance Requirements	Comments
Responsibility Centers (RCs)	T	T	P		L	Initial set-up could be high. Depends on degree of automation. RCs are needed to have costing and organizational reporting.
Literal designations (RC names)	T	T			L	Flexibility is needed since financial institutions reorganize often.
Organization codes (RC codes)	T	T			M	Same
Hierarchies (Summarization to upward organization hierarchy)	T	T			M	Same
Designation (cost center, service center, support center, overhead center, income center, and profit center)	T				L	Initial identification could require significant work. Depends on how many designations are to be used.

Figure 21 (Continued)

Legend—T = Typical Requirement; P = Possible Requirement; H = High; M = Medium; L = Low.

Specific Information to Be Maintained	Costing	Organizational Profitability	Product Profitability	Customer Profitability	Ongoing Maintenance Require-ments	Comments
Expense data by:						
RC	T	T	P		L	
Product	T	P	T		H	
Customer	P	P		T	M	
Budget	T	T	T	P		
Actual	T	T	T	T		
Forecast (Estimated actual)	P	T				
Revenue data by:						
RC	P	T	P		H	
Product	P	P	T		M	
Customer				T	H	
Budget	P	T	P	T		
Actual		T	T	T		
Forecast		T	P	T		

Figure 21 (Continued)

Legend—T = Typical Requirement; P = Possible Requirement; H = High; M = Medium; L = Low.

Specific Information to Be Maintained	Costing	Organizational Profitability	Product Profitability	Customer Profitability	Ongoing Maintenance Requirements	Comments
Relevant balance data by:						
RC	T	T	P		H	
Product	T	P	T	T	M	
Customer		P		T	H	
Budget	P	T	T			
Actual	T	T	T	T		
Forecast		T	T			
Relevant volume data by:						
Task	T				H	
Activity	T				H	
RC	T	T	P		M	
Product	T	P	T		M	
Customer				T	H	
Unit costs	T	P	T	T	H	Unit cost development and maintenance requires high level of resources.

Figure 21 (Continued)

Legend—T = Typical Requirement; P = Possible Requirement; H = High; M = Medium; L = Low.

Specific Information to Be Maintained	Costing	Organizational Profitability	Product Profitability	Customer Profitability	Ongoing Maintenance Require- ments	Comments
Overhead allocations, rates, algorithms	T	T	T	P	H	Level of effort depends on sophistication of system and automation.
Mapping (routing) of activities and products from one RC to others	T	P	T		M	Initial identification is high.
Funds transfer pricing (Funds valuation rates)	T	T	T	T	M/H	
Equity allocations		P			L/M	
Loan losses or reserves		P			L/M	
Transfer rates	T				M/H	

6

Asset and Liability Management

Today, asset and liability management (ALM) is one of the most important areas of earnings opportunity beckoning senior management in financial institutions. However, this area is not fully understood by some high level executives and can influence wide profit swings.

ALM deals with risks involving interest rates, liquidity, and capital adequacy. As far as earnings are concerned, interest-rate risk is the most important. Also, an interrelationship exists between interest-rate risk, liquidity risk, and credit risk.

In recent years, ALM has emerged as a critically important topic because of deregulation and increasing interest-rate volatility. Deregulation has forced financial institutions to pay interest on more deposits than they did previously. Rate volatility has become more of a problem since the early 1980s.

One way an institution can cope with interest-rate risk is to implement a vigorous ALM program. For such a program to be successful, senior officials must be committed to it and understand it, and they must make the right decisions in using it.

The objective of this chapter is to provide an overview of ALM so its importance and concepts can be understood easily. Included are suggestions on how to prepare and interpret ALM reports. Finally, some ideas on making decisions will be provided. How to set up and run an asset and liability committee (ALCO) also will be discussed.

Asset and Liability Management Defined

Asset and liability management (ALM) is a process in which a financial institution seeks to manage interest-rate risk, liquidity risk, and capital adequacy. ALM takes relevant factors affecting these risks into consideration and analyzes them for their impact. Some of the factors to consider in ALM are:

- The repricing opportunities of assets as loans mature or are prepaid.
- The repricing opportunities as liabilities mature.
- The impact of interest-rate changes on the institution's net interest margin.
- The need for additional funds.
- The institution's adequacy of capital to assets and liabilities.

Several issues underlie each of these considerations.

ALM coordinates the efforts of acquiring and deploying funds while focusing on earnings, liquidity, and capital issues. Analysis and decision making relies on the balance sheet and what it shows about income and sources and uses of funds. Also, interest-rate volatility has become an important factor in an institution's ability to maintain an adequate net interest margin.

ALM is a discipline for measuring, assessing, and managing interest-rate risk. When done properly, ALM tells managers where they are vulnerable and where they are well positioned.

Before we proceed further, it is important to define each of the risk elements that ALM addresses. The three discussed in this chapter are interest-rate risk, liquidity risk, and capital-adequacy risk.

Interest-Rate Risk

This risk is caused by changes in interest rates. It reflects an institution's volatility of earnings and market value resulting from interest-rate changes. This risk is one of the toughest confronting a financial institution.

Liquidity Risk

Liquidity risk represents the ability to satisfy commitments through a sufficiency of funds. The risk arises in having to borrow at a higher than normal interest rate to fund assets. An extreme case of liquidity risk has an institution relying on purchased funds and sale of assets to meet short-term obligations.

Capital Adequacy Risk

Capital adequacy risk involves having sufficient capital to leverage assets. Financial institutions often measure it as a ratio of capital to assets. For example, assume an institution's minimum requirement may be 7.5 percent of capital to assets. The idea is that the higher the ratio the healthier the institution.

In some institutions, the ratio also may be measured as capital to liabilities. State and federal regulators set minimum requirements on this ratio. There are prescribed risk-based capital ratios.

Operating and other losses and increased asset levels can depreciate the ratio.

One way that financial institutions manage this risk is by maintaining balance-sheet growth within the capital adequacy guidelines set by the regulators.

The Need for Asset and Liability Management

When properly executed, ALM provides an institution with a consistent net interest margin. It also prescribes liquidity and capital levels.

One of the major purposes of ALM is to minimize risk of earnings resulting from interest-rate changes. Other purposes include the following:

- Maintain a desired balance between interest-rate sensitive assets and interest-rate sensitive liabilities.
- Provide maximum net interest margins.
- Assure desired liquidity levels.
- Provide adequate cash flow.

- Maintain capital adequacy.

- Identify opportunities and contribute toward achieving ROA and ROE targets.

ALM is one key factor in maintaining financial stability. It provides tools to manage the controllable part of risk and can drive net income. ALM allows you to separate controllable from noncontrollable factors on the balance sheet. It also provides the tools to intelligently price controllable items to gain optimum net interest income.

For an institution to survive in today's highly volatile and competitive environment, a commitment to proactive asset and liability management is essential.

A good ALM program can result in the following:

- Stable net interest income.

- Higher return on assets.

- Higher return on equity.

- Optimal liquidity levels.

- Higher-than-normal capital adequacy.

An institution can realize great returns on the money it invests in ALM. When properly executed, ALM can be a profit generator.

An Overview of Conceptual Issues in Asset and Liability Management

Several issues confront the ALM practitioner. This sections covers briefly some of the most discussed ALM issues.

Tactical and Strategic Planning

An institution must not only know where it is going in the short term but also address long-term issues. Good ALM depends upon a good forward view on interest rates, liquidity, and capital adequacy, which are intertwined and jointly affect earnings.

Planning for the balance sheet composition is important. Deciding on a mix of variable rate mortgages to fixed rate mortgages is necessary. Also, levels of investments and cash must be decided. In the area of funding, issues ranging from the mix of deposits to purchased funds must be weighed against their impact on earnings and funding volatility.

Key questions in planning are:

1. Where does the institution want to be in the future with its balance-sheet mix?
2. How much interest-rate risk should the institution assume?
3. How much liquidity risk should the institution assume?
4. What are the threats to capital adequacy? How can they be controlled?

Planning drives the consideration of these issues to the here and now level. As institutions plan, they become aware of actions that must be initiated and addressed now.

Float

This is a common ALM issue. There are several kinds of float in an institution, some beneficial and some costly. Essentially, float is uncollected funds. The kinds of float confronting an institution include those shown in Figure 22.

One ALM issue is to keep the nonbeneficial float to a minimum. On a larger scale, an ALCO usually will oversee a funds control operation. Float control is a subset of this process. Funds control will be discussed in detail in the ALCO section later in this chapter.

How will the institution manage interest-rate risk? Several complementary processes can greatly enhance an institution's ability to manage the risk.

No single method will do the job totally. Several factors must be considered. First, gather good information; second, be able to analyze and interpret it accurately; and third, be able to take action that will lead to a desired level of risk.

Figure 22
Kinds of Float

	Definition	Example	Impact to Institution
			Beneficial (1) (+)	Non-Beneficial (2) (−)
Receiving Float	Institution receives instrument for collection. It must process the check and receives collected, usable funds after it clears. Book balance minus collected balance equals float.	Institution receives a check as a payment, exchange for cash or money order, for deposit.		−
Disbursing Float	Institution disburses instrument for collection. It retains the collected funds until the instrument is cleared via settlement with another institution.	Institution issues vendor payments such as payroll checks, or issues money orders or some other instrument.	+	

Notes:
(1) Creates soft interest income or reduces interest expense.
(2) Creates a funding cost to the institution.

Some institutions may desire to be as insulated as possible from interest-rate risk. However, they will have to pay a premium for hedging their position. In doing this, they must buy futures or options contracts that cover an opposite position from what they have in the marketplace. This way, if interest rates change they are covered in both directions, but it costs money to purchase the contracts.

They also can attempt to insulate themselves from interest-rate risk by structuring the balance sheet so as to minimize the effects of volatility in interest rates.

These methods cost money and tend to reduce net interest margins. Financial institutions usually choose a level of risk they feel comfortable with. Then they can control speculation. Contracts also can be used to speculate which direction rates will go.

The idea of ALM is to know the effect on net interest income when rates go up or down. Clearly, this is an important area and several factors can inhibit an institution's liquidity. For example, if an institution is heavily dependent on purchased funds and receives adverse publicity because of severe loan losses, it may find it difficult to purchase funds. Hence, a liquidity crisis could emerge. A good ALM would avert such a crisis through at least two preventative measures.

First, a good ALM program would recognize the dangers of a heavy dependency on purchased funds. There would be a policy against such a dependency. Second, ALM would establish a funding safety net. Some well-run institutions set up a funding contingency plan by establishing loan commitments with other financial institutions.

Liquidity is managed by analyzing the institution's position in the following:

- Historical funding patterns and requirements.

- Current liquidity position and requirements.

- Projected funding requirements.

The institution should review its options for attracting additional funds. Also, it should review ways to reduce funding requirements such as decreasing controllable nonliquid assets.

Options on funding include increasing term liabilities, short-term borrowings, short-term deposits, and capital.

Key to managing liquidity risk is forecasting accurately funding needs and events that will affect those needs. Also important is a contingency plan in case projections are wrong.

How will the institution maintain capital adequacy? This is a controlled process that must be monitored carefully. In an extreme case scenario, an institution is hit with unexpected huge loan losses and it ends up with a negative net worth. Capital adequacy here would be difficult to deal with. However, in an institution's normal course of operating, ALM seeks to maintain assets consistent with regulatory capital requirements.

ALM also seeks to optimize return on equity (ROE). Aside from fee income, this implies a leverage of equity to assets and its measured income. This performance measure must be closely watched.

The Analytical Tools of Asset and Liability Management—Overview

Some basic analytical tools are used in ALM. They include asset allocation, gap management, duration analysis, simulation, and optimization. Each approach has its usefulness and limitations and each deals with interest-rate risk in an unique way.

- Asset allocation is a method in which liabilities and capital are matched with assets according to interest rates and maturities. For example, capital would first be applied to fixed assets since both are long term and bear no interest. This method slots assets and liabilities into maturity buckets and seeks to explain their variances.

- Gap management assesses interest rate sensitivity according to maturities. This method is an improvement over basic asset allocation. It relies on a measure of rate sensitive assets to rate sensitive liabilities. Any resulting gaps are identified as repricing gaps. It also looks at funding surpluses and deficits in time buckets.

- Duration analysis looks at market price changes resulting from interest rate shifts. This technique seeks to measure an institution's value and shows value change as interest rates move.

- Simulation is a process of injecting "what-if" thinking and previewing the balance sheet based on scenarios. It is built around assumptions about interest rates and balances (volumes). This allows you to see the impact of alternatives before implementing them. Thus, you are predicting the future based on the possible outcome of your ideas.

- Optimization is probably the highest order of analysis in ALM. Optimization relies on such techniques as linear programming and is assisted at times by employing artificial intelligence. The analyst seeks to optimize the best possible combination of balances given certain assumptions on interest rates and balance velocities (volume). The idea is to gain optimal earnings by constructing the best combination of balances.

An ALM analyst defines the controllable variables and discovers ways to enhance earnings through the variables.

Let's look at each of these tools and explore them at greater length.

Asset Allocation

Asset allocation was an early ALM tool that sought to allocate funding sources to assets according to maturity, volatility, and market rates. This method has its advantages and disadvantages. It should not be used as the only ALM tool. If asset allocation is used it should be one of many ALM techniques. The advantage of asset allocation is that one can tie a funding source to assets and thereby simulate market reality in certain circumstances. A disadvantage arises when one attempts to perform ALM solely on the basis of asset allocation. This could lead to erroneous assumptions, because the cost of funds is emphasized instead of earnings.

Asset allocation focuses on maintaining liquidity. Therefore, its analysis process emphasizes availability of funds. This method generally would allocate funds as seen in Figure 23.

These allocations are arbitrary and represent one of many approaches to allocating sources to assets. The idea under this method is to convey the following:

1. Demand deposits can be spread to short- and long-term assets. A certain level of demand deposits is volatile to interest rate changes and therefore is considered short term.

2. Time deposits are considered longer-term funds in some cases; depending on stated maturity levels. You match these levels with the stated maturities of assets.

3. Purchased funds are volatile and should only be applied to short-term assets.

Figure 23
Asset Allocation Method

Sources (Liabilities and Capital) Uses (Assets)

	Amount	Fixed Assets	Other Nonearning	Cash and Due From	Loans Other Than Mortgages	Mortgage Loans	Short-Term and Marketable Securities and Investments	Total Assets
Demand Deposits	$ 400			100	200	50	50	400
Time Deposits	400		100		100	200		400
Purchased Funds	130				50		80	130
Equity (Capital)	70	70						70
Totals	$1,000	70	100	100	350	250	130	$1,000

4. Equity and capital should be assigned first to fixed assets. Next, they should be assigned to other nonearning assets and cash and due from.

The priorities for allocating funds are:

1. Allocate sources to fixed assets required to operate a financial institution. Examples include buildings, furniture, and equipment.

2. Next, allocate funds to cash, reserves, and correspondent institution accounts.

3. Next, allocate funds to secondary reserves according to maturity, variability of loans, and deposits. Investments are planned so they will mature when liquidity needs arise. Secondary reserves could include federal funds, certificates of deposit, and marketable securities, due within say five years.

From the standpoint of liquidity planning, asset allocation can be helpful. However, it must rely on the forecasts of dynamic rather than static events. Loan prepayments and early deposit withdrawals must be considered, based upon business cycles and seasonal variations. An institution's volatility to the market and other economics also must be eyed.

Nevertheless, this method has a drawback in prescribing liquidity intervention because it suggests that secondary reserves, including securities, be liquidated when interest rates rise. As rates rise the value of securities usually decreases. The idea is that when loan demand is high, securities must be liquidated to meet it. There is a correlation between loan demand and rising interest rates.

Asset allocation basically was contrived during a period in banking history when an abundance of free deposits existed and U.S. government securities (market value) were not vulnerable to interest rate changes.

Gap Management

Gap management is commonly used but is giving way to simulation and other methods. This method basically relies on constructing a repricing schedule for earning assets and funding liabilities within discrete time periods or buckets. For each period, liabilities subject to repricing are subtracted from the assets subject to repricing. The formula is: rate sensitive assets (RSAs) minus rate sensitive liabilities (RSLs) equals the interest rate sensitivity gap. If the result is a negative number, it means the institution is liability sensitive. This is because it has more liabilities sensitive to repricing in the indicated period than assets subject to repricing. Gap reports usually show the gap in two ways: One, on an incremental basis for each period; two, on a cumulative basis.

Figure 24 shows a simple gap report.

In Figure 24, the institution is liability sensitive in the first period (30 days or less). Use the formula RSAs minus RSLs = gap ($100–$125 = –$25). The negative gap means the institution has more liabilities subject to repricing in the period than assets. There are two reasons why this can be misleading. First, we don't know the detailed distribution and amounts for each day. For example, we could have all assets subject to repricing on day one and the liabilities spread evenly over the 30 days. Second, if the reported

Figure 24
Interest Rate Sensitivity Gap

Balances (Volume) Subject to Repricing

	Total	30 Days or Less	31 through 60 Days	61 through 180 Days	181 Days through One Year	Over One Year
Assets	$1,000	$100	$150	$100	$200	$450
Liabilities	1,000	125	100	80	250	445
Incremental Gap	—	<25>	50	20	<50>	5
Cumulative Gap	—	<25>	25	45	< 5>	0

volumes are based on contractual terms, we may not consider early prepayments of loans or early deposit withdrawals. Either of those could affect the repricing gap.

In the next time period (31 through 60 days), we have a positive gap: More assets are subject to repricing than liabilities ($150–$100 = $50). The cumulative gap is positive (–$25 + $50 = $25). Deciding on which time buckets to use for such things as demand deposits has to be resolved. One extreme is to put all demand deposits in the 30-day-or-less bucket. The other extreme is to put all of them in the one-year-or-more bucket. Whatever is decided should reflect reality. A gap report based on what really happens as opposed to what is prescribed by contractual arrangements will be more meaningful. A gap report that focuses on reality is called a managerial gap report.

Generally, an institution's gap position will indicate how direction changes in interest rates will affect net interest income. Figure 25 shows how net interest income can be influenced by changes in interest rates.

Let's explore briefly the implications of this grid. However, these are not absolutes because exceptions can occur.

1. When interest rates rise and there is a positive gap, then net interest income probably will increase. An institution

Figure 25
Net Interest Income Impact

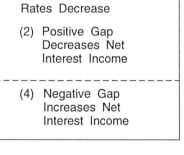

Interest Rates Increase	Interest Rates Decrease
(1) Positive Gap Increases Net Interest Income	(2) Positive Gap Decreases Net Interest Income
(3) Negative Gap Decreases Net Interest Income	(4) Negative Gap Increases Net Interest Income

in this quadrant has the ability to raise prices on earning assets faster than it has to raise interest rates on liabilities (deposits and other funds).

2. When interest rates decrease and there is a positive gap, then net interest income probably will decrease. This situation will likely depress earnings because the institution will have to reprice assets at lower interest rates before it can reprice liabilities at lower rates.

3. When interest rates increase and there is a negative gap, then net interest income likely will decrease. An institution in this quadrant has little flexibility. It must raise prices it pays for deposits and other funds before it can raise prices on loans.

4. When interest rates decrease and there is a negative gap, then net interest income probably will increase. An institution in this situation can lower prices on liabilities faster than it has to lower the prices on its assets, such as loans.

Advantages of Gap Management

- It measures accurately volumes of assets and liabilities that will become interest-rate sensitive.
- It is valuable for identifying balance sheet maturity areas vulnerable to unfavorable interest rate movements.

Disadvantages, Limitations, and Cautions of Gap Management

- It doesn't measure the risk attributed to varied rate curves of each product.
- It has at least nominally outlived its usefulness. Rates are too volatile for gap management to be reliable. The magnitude of interest-rate risk can be underestimated when gap reports are used.
- Its theory assumes repricing will follow the direction of rates. For example, declining rates correlate with declining prices. This isn't always true.

- It relies heavily on assumption that repricing timing is the dominant factor affecting interest-rate risk, and, hence, net interest income. Repricing only opens windows of opportunity. Therefore, it isn't as influential as much as some might suggest.

- If it is based strictly on contractual terms, gap management ignores prepayment of loans and early withdrawals.

- It may ignore the lead/lag effect of interest-rate changes.

- It assumes that a zero gap will produce stable earnings, but this may not be true. A zero gap even could depress earnings.

- It is not absolute and could therefore distort the earnings outlook. For example, it is possible to be in a liability sensitivity position during declining rates and have your net interest margin decline as well.

- It ignores spread risk and cash flows.

- Time buckets could distort conclusions if the underlying details are not known.

Preparing a Gap Report

A gap analysis report provides a measurement of repricing velocity of assets and liabilities. The report cites velocity over specified periods, for example, 30, 60, or 90 days. Because risk occurs within 30 days, some financial institutions prepare gap reports for periods of less than 30 days.

The report usually is formatted to categorize assets and liabilities. They are spread out so that segments subject to interest-rate change are slotted by time horizon and amount. Also, the interest-rate base for each amount is listed. The base rate determines the scale at which assets and liabilities are being repriced.

The idea is to compare for each period the assets available for repricing to the liabilities available for repricing. This provides a determination of the net interest-rate risk inherent in the balance sheet.

Several things can be done with a gap report, including taking action, identifying opportunities, and monitoring balance sheet behavior.

The following chart summarizes these kinds of activities:

Activity	Action	Opportunity	Monitor	Short Term	Longer Term
Deposit Pricing	X			X	
Loan Pricing	X			X	X
Investments	X	X		X	
Portfolio Structuring	X	X			X
Market Values			X		X

A gap report can be as detailed as you wish. It depends largely on what information is available and what you plan to do with it. Generally, the more you can understand the underlying details of your balance sheet the more useful your gap report will be.

Figure 26 is a simplified example of a gap report. A more detailed report would show more categories and would show time intervals beyond one year.

In Figure 26, the 0–30 day intervals shows a liability sensitive financial institution. That is, it has more liabilities than assets maturing for repricing. The negative gap is $32,200. In the 61–90 day interval, $1,700 in assets match the $1,700 in liabilities due for repricing. The gap is zero.

A gap report really can be viewed and constructed in two basic ways. They are contractual and managerial. A contractual gap report is objective, with its construction based on stated maturities. This is the kind of report regulators usually ask for.

It is used for external purposes. Internal management can't use it because it doesn't reflect what could really happen. A contractual gap report has the following characteristics:

- It is based on period-end balances.

Figure 26
Maturity and Rate Sensitivity Analysis

Interval (in Days)

	Rate	Total Balance	0–30	31–60	61–90	91–180	181–365	>1 Year
Interest-Earning Assets								
Investments	10.00%	$ 5,000	$ 1,000	0	0	$ 1,500	$ 800	$ 1,700
Real Estate Loans								
Fixed	11.50	20,000	300	200	600	400	700	17,800
Variable	11.00	25,000	500	700	600	18,000	2,400	2,800
Commercial (Prime Rate)	10.50	5,000	1,500	2,500	500	500	0	0
Total	11.05	$55,000	$ 3,300	$3,400	$1,700	$20,400	$3,900	$22,300
Interest-Bearing Liabilities								
Money Market Deposits	7.00	30,000	30,000	0	0	0	0	0
Savings Deposits	5.50	10,000	1,000	800	1,100	900	1,500	4,700
Time Deposits	10.00	12,000	1,500	1,000	600	400	1,700	6,800
Purchased Funds	11.50	3,000	3,000	0	0	0	0	0
Total	7.63	$55,000	$35,500	$ 1,800	$ 1,700	$ 1,300	$ 3,200	$11,500
Spread	3.42%							
Maturity Gap			<32,200>	1,600	0	19,100	700	10,800
Cumulative Gap			<32,200>	<30,600>	<30,600>	<11,500>	<10,800>	0

- It reflects stated maturities of fixed-rate items.
- It recognizes repricing of variable rate accounts.
- It includes any effects resulting from swaps, futures, and options.
- It ignores prepayment options.

Conversely, a managerial gap report is subjective and looks at what really could happen.

It is designed for internal management use and its characteristics:

- Take into account loan prepayments.
- Take into account early withdrawals.
- Consider volatility of core deposits, e.g., demand deposit accounts, which are subject to seasonal factors.

Part of the analysis compares the institution's gap position in a given period with predicted interest rate levels. The result is a framework for estimating the effect of this relationship on net interest income.

Gap analysis should not be the only tool used. If used by itself, a financial institution could be led into bad decisions.

Gap analysis can provide a basis for deploying tactics. Here are two possibilities:

- If interest rates are perceived to be rising, the gap is characteristically altered by converting fixed-rate assets into variable-rate assets and variable-rate liabilities into fixed-rate liabilities. This results in a higher asset interest-rate sensitivity. The implication is that you have an increased opportunity to reprice assets and thereby take advantage of higher pricing resulting from higher rates.
- If interest rates are perceived to be declining, the gap is changed by converting variable-rate assets into fixed-rate assets and fixed-rate liabilities into variable-rate liabilities. This results in a higher liability interest-rate sensitivity. The implication is that you have a greater opportunity to reprice liabilities at lower interest rates.

For example, assume the previous gap report showed that total rate sensitive assets (RSAs) and rate sensitive liabilities (RSLs) are matched. The gap is zero. Also, RSAs ÷ RSLs equals 1. As far as gap analysis goes, this is the total of most financial institutions, but be cautious here. Suppose a financial institution has a zero gap (RSA–RSLs=0) in each interval (time) bucket using contractual (objective gap). Also it has loans with prepayment options. If rates go up, the institution will not be adversely affected. But if rates fall substantially, it could suffer.

The idea behind gap management is not to rely totally on managing gaps; total return-based measures should also be used. Gap management is only one of many tools used in trying to manage net interest income.

Duration Analysis

Duration analysis considers the cash flow and market value of a financial instrument. The analysis is used to determine the change in market value (price) of an instrument as interest rates move. When rates go up, the value of assets goes down. The analysis also measures the possible change in net worth resulting from interest-rate changes. Duration analysis further provides an estimate of the weighted average maturity of an instrument or a total portfolio.

Duration analysis provides information leading to matching durations of assets and liabilities. By matching durations, an institution can immunize an instrument or portfolio from both market value risk and reinvestment risk. The idea is that when durations are matched, rate changes cause shifts in market values, and reinvestments must be made to offset (assets to liabilities) because they move in opposite directions.

Advantages of Duration Analysis

- It provides a long-term focus of rate-change effects on earnings.
- It provides information tools that could immunize net worth from interest-rate risk. Immunization occurs when the duration of assets is equal to the duration of liabilities.

- It incorporates interest cash flow.

- It provides useful information for long-term pricing.

Weaknesses and Disadvantages of Duration Analysis

- It does not adequately deal with variable rate instruments by carrying the assumption that rates will be uniform over the life of an instrument.

- It emphasizes the long-term impact on earnings but ignores the short-term.

- It does not apply to all rate-sensitive assets and liabilities.

- Estimates of prepayments for the analysis may be difficult.

- Estimates of liquidity of deposits for the analysis may be difficult.

- The portfolio duration may shift and have to be rebalanced or recalibrated, a complex process.

- Duration assumes that rates on the yield curve will rise or fall at the same rate. For example, if rates generally rise by 1.5 percentage points, duration assumes all rates, short and long term, will rise equally.

Using a bond as an example, duration analysis shows the value change of the bond as interest rates move. Figure 27 shows how to calculate the duration of a bond.

It is possible to have a $1 million bond with the same duration as a $1,000 bond. This is because duration measures estimated average maturity, discounted period numbers, rather than cash flows. To match liquidity and maturity, the analyst must have similar cash flows for assets and liabilities.

An instrument with a duration of four years is twice as sensitive to interest-rate changes as one with a duration of two years.

Generally, the following occurs: the longer the maturity and the lower the interest rate, the higher the duration. A higher duration results in a greater interest-rate risk. The shorter the maturity

Figure 27
Duration of Five-Year, 10 Percent $1,000 Bond (Priced at Par)

(1)	(2)	(3)	(4)	(5)	(6)
Year	Cash Flow	Present Value (PV) @10%	PV of Cash Flow (Col. 2 × Col. 3)	PV ÷ Price at Par	Contribution of Cash Flow (Col. 1 × Col. 5)
1	$ 100	0.909	$ 90.90	.0909	.0909
2	100	0.827	82.70	.0827	.1654
3	100	0.751	75.10	.0751	.2253
4	100	0.683	68.30	.0683	.2732
5	1,100	0.621	683.00	.6830	3.4150
Totals	$1,500	—	$1,000.00	1.0000	4.1698

Duration=4.17 years.

and the higher the interest rate, the lower the duration. A lower duration results in less interest-rate risk.

In the example of a 5-year $1,000 (at par) bond at 10 percent with one payment a year, the calculated duration is 4.17 years. Suppose the current market rate or yield for a comparable bond is 11 percent. By using a modified duration formula, we can calculate the effects of interest rate changes on the value of this fixed-rate instrument. The modified duration formula is as follows:

Modified Duration = Duration − (1 ÷ Market Yield ÷ Number of Cash Flows Per Year)

The Calculation:

- Modified duration = 4.17 years ÷ (1 + 11% ÷ 1)
- Modified duration = 4.17 years ÷ 1.11
- Modified duration = 3.757 years

Now suppose you want to determine the shift in value of the bond as interest rates change further. And interest rates are expected to rise another 1.5 percentage points. The following formula will help you to determine the value change:

$$\begin{array}{l}\text{Market Value Percentage}\\ \text{Change for Fixed Rate}\\ \text{Instrument}\end{array} = \begin{array}{l}\text{Modified}\\ \text{Duration} \times \text{Change}\\ \text{in Market Yield}\end{array}$$

$$\text{Market Value Percentage Change} =$$
$$3.757 \text{ Years} \times 1.5 \text{ Percentage Points}$$

$$\text{Market Value Percentage Change} = 5.636 \text{ Percent}$$

In this example, if interest rates rise 1.5 percentage points, the bond would decline 5.6 percent in value.

Duration provides an accurate measure of market value given interest-rate risk. When interest rates fall, a fixed-rate loan or other fixed-rate asset will rise in value. However, the cash flow received from the assets will have to be reinvested at lower rates. The reverse occurs when interest rates rise. When rates rise a fixed-rate loan or other fixed-rate assets will decline in value. The cash flow received from these assets can be reinvested at higher rates, however.

Duration helps you to focus on unrealized gains and losses resulting from changes in market value as interest rates move. Duration will not stabilize net interest income. But it helps an institution to stabilize unrealized gains and losses.

Simulation

In simulation you use your ideas to predict what earnings might be in the future under certain conditions. In effect, you are previewing tomorrow's financial statements. This process helps the A/L analyst to estimate the effect of certain changes on earnings. One of the processes is to "disaggregate" the balance sheet into microcosms of rates and terms so you can separate controllable from noncontrollable items. In separating the controllable items, the impact of pricing on earnings can be determined.

Thus, simulation provides the kind of analysis needed up front for decision making. The goal is simulation is to surmise the impact of decisions before you make them.

In "disaggregating" your balance sheet try to sort out what really will happen (managerial) from what is defined to happen (contractual). For example, in a managerial analysis, loans prepayments have more influence and make more sense than amortizations (contractual).

In simulation, look at the timing of pricing opportunities and the impact of rates. The idea is to simulate ways to shelter earnings given scenarios of rising, flat, or falling rates. Essentially, simulation is a form of profit planning. In fact, during the profit planning cycle, a rate simulation is usually done. In A/L management, rate simulations are done frequently.

The simulation process depends on the expertise of the analysts and requires much detailed data.

Figure 28 is an example of a decision matrix with an analysis of funding strategies and interest rate scenarios. It shows the net result of many detailed calculations. Several microcomputer models on the market can provide this kind of analysis.

One technique used includes Monte-Carlo simulation. This can be used to analyze mortgage pool behavior, estimate option adjusted spreads, and ascertain core deposits and their behavior.

Fractuals theory and Fuzzy logic (engineering) are other models. They are concerned with formal principles of approximate reasoning, which have neither linear nor deterministic expression. These models can be used to help manage uncertainty connected to the amount of funds (by source) and their usage. Exchange rate analysis can also be done using these techniques.

Figure 28
Projected Change in Net Interest Income for 12 Months

Funding Strategies (Maturity)

Rate Scenarios	Shorten	Status Quo	Extend
Rising	<$1>	$4	$6
Flat	$2	0	<$3>
Declining	$5	<$3>	<$7>
Most Likely	$3	$1	<$4>
Worst Case	$1	<$1>	<$3>

In addition, there is Chaos theory and Swarm theory. The Chaos theory origin comes from the thought that if a system consisted of a few parts that interacted strongly, it could exhibit unpredictable behavior. The object is to study the irregular behavior of simple deterministic equations by providing more sophisticated tools that are closer to real life. It provides a means for marking valid opportunity identifications. The study of chaos reveals hidden patterns of order fluctuations that quite often characterize complex systems such as the stock market. Nonlinear approaches to short-term forecasting employ chaotic attractors, making it possible to predict incipient crises. This provides prediction capabilities to financial instruments, making it possible to reach a high degree of significance in terms of predictability.

Swarm theory uses a highly complex econometric model. By use of a swarm model one can map the market and its complex structure of independent agents. It has the ability to take community behavior and emulate an economy as a swarm of economic and financial agents. The goal is to bring into the model market psychology and its undercurrents. The goal of forecasting market behavior through community intelligence, such as swarms, is to provide an analytical infrastructure permitting the maximization of returns while reducing the risk relative to investment objectives. As economic conditions, financial instruments, and most importantly market psychology change, the investment mix has to be managed to reflect not-so-clear goals and evolving market conditions.

Nonetheless, funding strategies are not necessarily symmetrical in their impact on interest income. A rate direction is not always of the same magnitude as the opposite change. Changing rates and spreads can be asymmetrical given certain interest-rate directions and maturities. In Figure 27, we see that a flat rate scenario produces a $2 increase in interest income when liability maturities are shortened. However, a $3 decrease results when maturities are extended. Obviously, the undisclosed factor is how much in volume and balance does the "shorten," "extend," rise, and decline represent.

The advantage of simulation is the kind of "what-if" information it provides, projecting what will happen under certain conditions.

A key disadvantage is that it demands detailed information, which can be time consuming to gather.

Optimization

This approach is advancing the state-of-the-art in asset and liability management. Linear programming is one technique being used to solve the optimal balance-sheet mix. Artificial Intelligence (AI) through artificial neural networks is being used in optimization calculations and analyses. For example, this provides tools for currency exchange rate forecasting.

The goal is to optimize net interest income given certain rate assumptions and funding constraints. With the use of linear programming, one can isolate the optimum mix. It appears the more homogeneous a portfolio the more useful optimization is as a modeling technique. It should not, however, be used in isolation because it does not consider dynamic occurrences.

Another technique for optimizing the use of resources is differential equations through dynamic programming. Genetic Algorithms are looked at as a possible method for solving combinatorial type optimization problems. Genetic Algorithms employ trial and error in a direct analogy to how the biological process of mutation works. For each iterative solution a fitness criterion is used. This is a highly iterative process and is not a bad way to search in a solution space. The difficulty with Genetic Algorithms is to define fitness, a process that can be tricky because to a large extent it is subjective. One of the risks, for instance, is that one can overrate the data. Optimization applications using Genetic Algorithms include foreign exchange operations, off-balance sheet operations, and capital market forecasts.

Establishing and Operating an Asset and Liability Committee (ALCO)

In some institutions, the ALCO meets weekly and has wide authority. In others, it may meet monthly and serve as an advisory panel to the CEO, COO, or CFO. Either way, the ALCO's purpose and charter must be clearly defined and understood.

A set of objectives resulting from strategic planning may set in motion the formation of an ALCO. Objectives such as the ratio of rate-sensitive assets (RSAs) to rate-sensitive liabilities (RSLs) may be stated explicitly. It is up to the ALCO to find ways to achieve the objectives.

A successful ALCO program is the result of an active management. The ALCO must select strategies that provide acceptable earnings under the most probable future conditions.

ALCO Charter and Policy

One of the first things an ALCO must do is write a charter and policy statement. A charter may follow this general outline:

   I. Purpose and Function
   II. Goals and Objectives
   III. Membership and Authority
   IV. Agenda and Duties
   V. Policy and Guidelines

Take each outline item and look at the possibilities.

I. Purpose and Function

A clear definition on why the committee exists and what it will do must be stated explicitly. Also, a charter statement such as, "The ALCO exists to optimize the earnings of the institution," could be part of this section. An ALCO will manage within the framework of stated strategies and constraints. An expectation of performance also is stated.

II. Goals and Objectives

The committee may specify that certain goals and objectives prevail as a result of the institution's overall strategic plan. The following, some the result of policy, are examples of ALCO goals:

- Maintain an interest margin (spread) of 5.5 percent to 6.0 percent.
- Achieve a return on assets (ROA) target of 1.25 percent.
- Achieve a return on equity (ROE) target of 18 percent.
- Maintain an equity capital ratio to assets of 10 percent.
- Maintain a loan portfolio to equal 50 to 65 percent of total assets.
- Maintain rate-sensitive assets (RSAs) to rate-sensitive liabilities (RSLs) within a 10 percent variance from one another.
- Maintain a liquidity ratio at 20 percent.

III. Membership and Authority

Depending on management philosophy and size of the institution, the following officials should be members of the ALCO:

- Chief executive officer (CEO)
- Chief operating officer (COO)
- Chief financial officer (CFO)
- Controller
- Treasurer
- Chief credit officer (lending)
- Head of operations (float, logistics)
- Chief investment officer (investments)
- Head of retail banking (deposits)
- International banking chief

The idea is to have individuals on the committee who represent functions critical to achieving the goals and objectives of the ALCO. Each official must be committed to carrying out the ALCO charter and be willing to participate. The committee membership should be five to seven persons. Authority over performance of specific accountabilities should be stated explicitly.

IV. Agenda and Duties

In addition to specifying the ALCO agenda for each meeting, a statement should say who is accountable for preparing and presenting each item. An agenda may include:

1. Review economic environment (rates, inflation, economy, foreign exchange—if applicable).
2. Review interest rate forecasts.
3. Review plan to actual performance (loan volume, margins, balance-sheet mix). Prepare revised forecasts.
4. Review and approve A and L pricing committee recommendations.
5. Review the institution's liquidity position.
6. Review the institution's capital position.
7. Review the maturity distribution assets and liabilities.
8. Review the contingency funding plan (funding safety net and asset contraction plan).
9. Review alternative funding sources for the lowest possible cost.
10. Review duration analysis.
11. Review interest rate simulation.
12. Review mismatches between RSAs and RSLs (gaps).
13. Review nonearning assets, including nonperforming loans.
14. Review cash and due from balances.
15. Review float position.
16. Review anticipated changes in balance-sheet mix of loans, nonearning assets, investments, and sources of funds.
17. Review portfolio strategies on loans, investments, and sources of funds.
18. Review tax issues.
19. Each quarter, review performance against other banks on margins, ROA, ROE, ROEA, capital adequacy, loans to assets, and liquidity.

V. Policy and Guidelines

In establishing policy and guidelines, one must recognize that decisions to capture immediate short-term earnings could reduce future earnings. Therefore, this section should include policies and guidelines that address such issues. For example, a statement should be included saying: "Each decision should be tested for its tactical (short-term) and strategic (long-term) impact."

This section also should state policies and guidelines that reinforce the importance of maintaining or achieving such goals as earnings stability. Also needed are statements of philosophy such as management's belief in not getting the institution into unnecessary market speculation. Therefore, risk guidelines are vital. There should be an explicit statement on the exposure of interest-rate risk the institution is willing to undertake. Additionally, this section could state policies and guidelines for lending, funding, pricing, investments, and hedging.

For an ALCO to be effective, its members must have credibility and their actions easily understood. The committee's reports should be focused with information rather than just burdened with data. Each ALCO member should be accountable for action items at each meeting. The members will use the meeting to focus on opportunities for increasing net interest income by maintaining healthy liquidity and capital adequacy and lowering interest-rate risk.

An effective ALCO will know where balance sheet risks are and what to do to minimize risk while optimizing net interest income.

Factors to Consider in Acquiring or Developing an Asset and Liability Management Model

Many institutions choose to purchase and install an outside vendor package for performing their asset and liability management analyses and generating reports. Others develop an in-house system.

A checklist to consider in evaluating or specifying a software model consists of:

Purchase price or cost to develop.
Hardware requirements.
Vendor installation support.
Vendor training.
Vendor availability for consultation.
Vendor reputation with clients.
Vendor maintenance.
Vendor updates.
Mainframe download capability.
Industry specific.

Reports:

Gap (static, dynamic, and cumulative).
Budget to actual.
Cash flow.
Earnings.
Duration analysis.
Simulation capability (multiple scenarios, rates, balances, and maturities).
Storage of historical data.
Number of interest rate categories.
User defined rate categories (yes, no).
Number of account categories (A/L).
User defined account categories (yes, no).
Number of time periods for planning and capability.
Loan and deposit maturity and repricing capability.
Amortization capability.
Loan repayment capability.
Download acceptance of interest rate projections.
Tax planning.
Consolidation from several reporting entities.
Capability.
Help screens.
Preview screen before printing reports.
Graphics.

In going through a requirements definition, additional items may arise.

Summary

The main goal of asset and liability management (ALM) is to optimize net interest income while minimizing liquidity risk, capital-adequacy risk, and interest-rate risk. Here, management's participation and commitment can pay large returns.

One of the goals of an ALM practitioner is to provide credible and easy to understand information as a basis for informed decision making. An ALM practitioner must understand not only the analytical tools available and their uses but also their limitations.

The state-of-the-art in ALM is increasing daily in sophistication. At a minimum, senior management has to understand the basics of ALM and how it can benefit an institution through areas of focus using gap, duration, simulation, and optimization techniques. See Figure 29.

Figure 29
Areas of Focus

Technique	Liquidity	Interest-Rate Risk	Market Value	Earnings
Asset Allocation	X			
Gap	X	X		X
Duration	X	X	X	
Simulation				X
Optimization				X

7

Performance and Risk Measurement Reporting

This chapter provides a capstone on what to report in measuring performance and risk. Several report formats and key performance indicators (KPIs) are provided. The goal here is to show how information can be presented to top management with the following features (see Figures 30-39):

> Key Performance Indicators
> Early Warning Flags (risk)
> Exceptions
> Financial Highlights
> Graphs

Top management needs information that reports performance by organization, product, and major customer segments. Management also needs information that alerts it to risk. Some of the common risks include interest-rate risk, liquidity risk, credit quality risk, foreign exchange risk, transfer risk, and operating or snafu risk.

Throughout this chapter, emphasis will be on providing focused and relevant information that top management can read easily and understand.

Top Management Reports

Management philosophy often determines what to report, how frequently, and how detailed to report it. If you start at the top and zero in on the board, CEO, COO, and CFO, you probably have settled on the most essential areas for information needs. As you cascade down in the organization, peel-back reports providing more details should be available. Top management's need for information has a way of driving the entire information reporting system. Top managers' needs force information to build from bottom to top.

Executives usually have little time for details. When an exception or unusual circumstance arises they may seek more information. Therefore, high-level summary information usually meets the needs of top management. Certainly, each top manager must be informed of all relevant factors pertaining to his or her accountability; but each doesn't have to see all the details.

Two basic management styles exist when it comes to use of information. One style is the decisive manager who requires brevity. This person makes decisions without wading through piles of information. He or she uses some information but relies on intuitive thinking and experience to support decisions. Therefore, only summary information may be required. The other type of manager is the integrative manager who likes to review much data before making decisions. This person usually requires details. A good information system must be flexible enough to balance the needs of both management styles. The challenge is to meet the needs of the prevailing style and be flexible when it changes.

Examples of the report in this chapter for brevity sake are directed toward a "decisive" management style. This does not preclude the practitioner from developing detailed peel-back reports. In fact, a basis is provided later for determining what details are needed to report summary information.

The following is an example of a top-management information and control-report package. Depending on an institution's size and business orientation, its contents will vary. Experience indicates that usually the CFO's office prepares these kinds of reports. Some are prepared monthly; others, quarterly. Again, the level of detail will depend on the prevailing management style. The audience for this kind of report may include the board of directors, CEO, COO, and other officers of the management committee.

This report package evolves and undoubtedly its contents in time will change. It should provide a high-level report of what is occurring in an institution. Top management needs to see clear, concise, and relevant information so it can focus on pertinent issues. Therefore, stray data is taboo. The idea is not to distract the reader with nonessential information. To a certain point, the fewer the pages in the package the better, and the number of variables cited should be kept to a minimum. Don't overwhelm your audience with excess data. Give the information focus so management will be able to grasp it and probe for further understanding. The more concise the information, the more relevant it will be.

One factor is to keep in mind in developing a package that will be seen by the board is its members' usual diversity of backgrounds. A board normally has members from different professions, vocations, and businesses. Each member will have a different perspective.

Other reports could include:

- A list of scheduled items of classified assets, including other real estate that is owned.

- Organization (business entity) profitability.

- Product profitability.

Financial Highlights and Key Performance Indicators

Financial highlights (Figure 30) and key performance indicators page(s) are designed to give management a quick overview of performance and risk. Enough information should be provided to prompt such questions as: (1) Can costs be reduced? (2) Should our marketing strategy be changed? (3) Can unprofitable business be eliminated? (4) Can revenue be increased? An effective peel-back reporting system would answer these specific questions. A unified reporting system would align itself to questions that follow:

Questions	Answers
Can costs be reduced?	
Which ones?	Details of expenses with flags on excesses.

Management Control

Questions	Answers
Which units are not controlling costs?	Details of units not conforming to budgetary constraints.
Should marketing strategy be changed?	
What types of business should be promoted?	Profile of market share and business opportunities.
	Product profitability reports.
Can unprofitable business be eliminated?	
What is the financial impact to the institution?	Product profitability reporting.
Can revenue be increased?	
What are the products?	Pricing committee strategy and review program.
Where are fee increases needed?	Cost data, market research data.

This information should be available on request but should not be part of the top management report.

Brief Narrative of Operating Results and Exceptions

This page (Figure 30) should provide a brief narrative of key items, exceptions, highlights, initiatives, and changes. It should explain

---

Figure 30
Table of Contents

---

any unusual events. Significant unusual occurrences would be stated on the financial highlights and key performance indicators page(s). Short bullet statements of these occurrences should be noted.

Graphs

Some measures can be reported on graphs (Figures 31 through 36). What to report depends on the institution's business orientation, problem, or business focus. A plan-to-actual comparison helps management to maintain control. A subjective evaluation such as good, medium, or bad allows for some interpretation. It helps management by directing its focus to trends and areas needing extra attention. The broad subject areas of performance, loans, funding, liquidity, interest rates, capital adequacy, and asset and liability management provide a comprehensive overview of performance and major risk.

Income Statement

A summary (one page) income statement (Figure 37) should suffice for an overview. Top management does not need to see every line item. The idea is to list what is important. Further details, such as organizational (business entity) profitability reporting, can be set out in subsequent pages.

The income statement provides trend information, plan-to-actual performance, and tells whether it is favorable or unfavorable. In reporting trend information, the benefit of comparing this month to last month is the ability to spot significant variations.

Consolidated Balance Sheet

The intent of providing a balance sheet (Figure 38) is to update the financial condition from last month and to highlight changes. List only those categories that are significant. Small balances should be lumped together.

Credit Risk

Because credit risk (Figure 39) is crucial, several report pages may be used to show it in different dimensions: risk by industry, country, region, loan category, and lending responsibility center. Don't list individual delinquent borrowers here. However, they should

Figure 31
Financial Highlights for the Month of January 19XX
($ in 000's)

Financial Highlights	This Month Actual	Last Month Actual	Change from Last Month	F/U	This Month Plan	This Month Variance from Plan	F/U	YTD Actual	YTD Plan	YTD Variance from Plan	F/U
Operating Revenue											
Interest Revenue on Loans	851.1	840.0	11.1	F	860.0	-8.9	U	851.1	860.0	-8.9	U
Interest Revenue on Investments	61.0	60.0	1.0	F	61.0	0	F	61.0	61.0	0	F
Interest on Funds Placed	93.3	93.0	.3	F	94.0	-.7	U	93.3	94.0	-.7	U
Interest on Lease Financing	22.4	23.0	-.6	U	23.0	-.6	U	22.4	23.0	-.6	U
Total Interest Income	1,027.8	1,016.0	11.8	F	1,038.0	-10.2	U	1,027.8	1,038.0	-10.2	U
Net Interest Expense	431.4	430.0	1.4	U	439.0	-7.6	F	431.4	439.0	-7.6	F
Net Interest Income	596.4	586.0	10.4	F	599.0	-2.6	U	596.4	599.0	-2.6	U
Provision for Loan & Lease Losses	58.0	58.0	0	F	58.0	0	F	58.0	58.0	0	F
Net Interest Income after Provision for Losses	538.4	528.0	10.4	F	541.0	-2.6	U	538.4	541.0	-2.6	U
Fee Income	47.2	50.0	-2.8	U	47.0	.2	F	47.2	47.0	.2	F
Other Income	8.0	8.0	0	F	8.0	0	F	8.0	8.0	0	F
Total Operating Income	593.6	586.0	7.6	F	596.0	-2.4	U	593.6	596.0	-2.4	U

Year-to-Date (YTD)

Figure 31 (Continued)

Financial Highlights	This Month Actual	Last Month Actual	Change from Last Month	F U	This Month Plan	This Month Variance from Plan	F U	YTD Actual	YTD Plan	YTD Variance from Plan	F U
Operating Expense											
Personnel Expense	264.0	280.0	−16.0	F	264.0	0	F	264.0	264.0	0	F
Other Operating Expense	222.3	235.0	−12.7	F	222.0	.3	U	222.3	222.0	.3	U
Total Operating Expense	486.3	515.0	−28.7	F	486.0	.3	U	486.3	486.0	.3	U
Earnings—Subsidiaries	2.1	10.1	−8.0	U	5.0	−2.9	U	2.1	5.0	−2.9	U
Net Operating Income/(Loss) before Tax	109.4	81.1	28.3	F	115.0	−5.6	U	109.4	115.0	−5.6	U
Nonoperating Revenue	38.3	0	38.3	F	0	38.3	F	38.3	0	38.3	F
Nonoperating Expense	4.5	0	4.5	U	0	4.5	U	4.5	0	4.5	U
Nonoperating Income	33.8	0	33.8	F	0	33.8	F	33.8	0	33.8	F
Earnings/(Loss) before Taxes	143.2	81.1	62.1	F	115.0	28.2	F	143.2	115.0	28.2	F
Taxes/(benefit)	57.3	32.4	24.9	U	46.0	11.3	U	57.3	46.0	11.3	U
Earnings/(Loss) after Taxes	85.9	48.7	37.2	F	69.0	16.9	F	85.9	69.0	16.7	F
Earnings/Per share (Loss)	$.072	$.041	$.031	F	$.058	$.014	F	$.072	$.058	$.014	F

F = Favorable
U = Unfavorable

Figure 32
Brief Narrative and Summary

- Key Items
- Exceptions
- Highlights
- Initiatives
- Changes

(Brief bullet statements)

---

be listed in a peel-back report. The board package also could contain optional pages for special purposes.

Personnel Status

On the average, 50 percent of a financial institution's noninterest expense is related to personnel. Therefore, this report is an important control tool for keeping staffing within budget guidelines. How many responsibility centers to list is determined by the institution's size and management style. Summarizing 20 to 25 organization units is probably more than necessary in this report. Certainly details on roll-up organizations should be available on request.

Asset and Liability Management

Nothing exotic or complicated should be reported here. Top management's understanding of asset and liability management may be basic at best. Therefore, useful basic information should be provided. At a minimum, however, executives should be provided with information on average balances, yields, rates, and maturities.

Subsidiaries—Earnings and Activities

If the institution has any subsidiaries, they should be reported here. A brief presentation of earnings and activities should be cited.

Figure 33
Trend Graphs—Performance

Performance

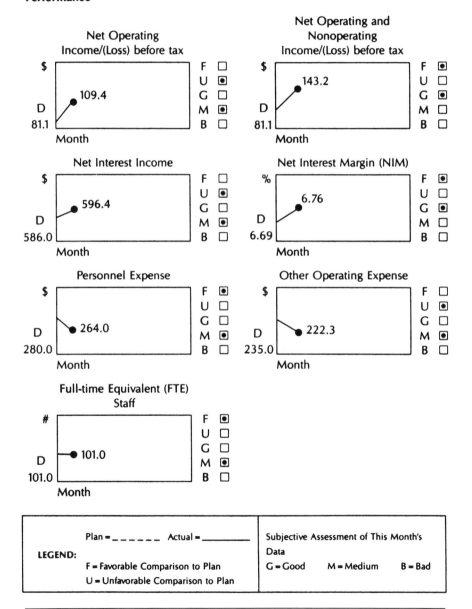

Figure 33 (Continued)

Performance

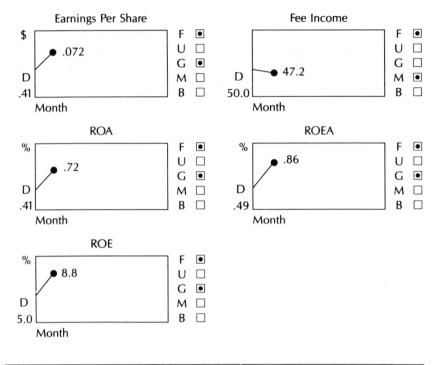

Figure 34
Trend Graphs—Loans

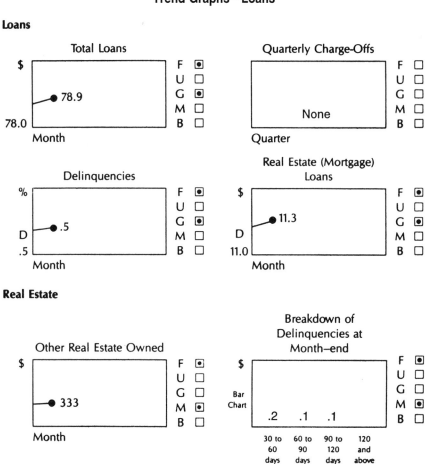

Loans

Total Loans

Quarterly Charge-Offs

Delinquencies

Real Estate (Mortgage) Loans

Real Estate

Other Real Estate Owned

Breakdown of Delinquencies at Month–end

157

Figure 35
Trend Graphs—Funding and Liquidity

Funding

Current Month Funding Mix

% Mix		F ▣
30	Demand	
15	Savings Accounts	U ☐
10	Jumbo CDs	G ☐
20	Other CDs	M ▣
15	Borrowed Money	B ☐
10	Brokered Deposits	

Liquidity Projections

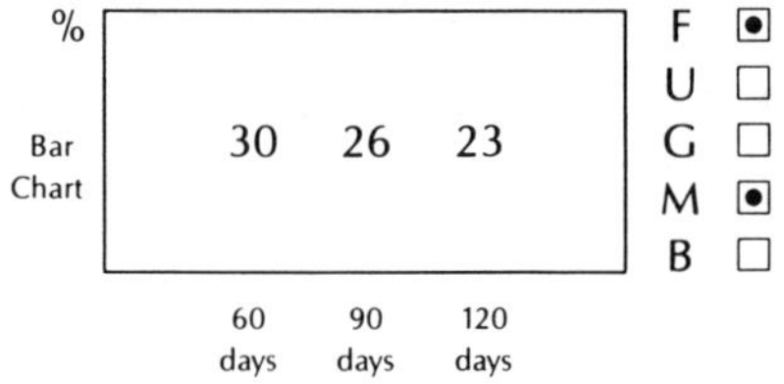

%   F ▣
     U ☐
Bar   30 26 23   G ☐
Chart   M ▣
                   B ☐

60   90   120
days days days

Liquidity

Cash and Marketable
Investments/Securities to
Assets

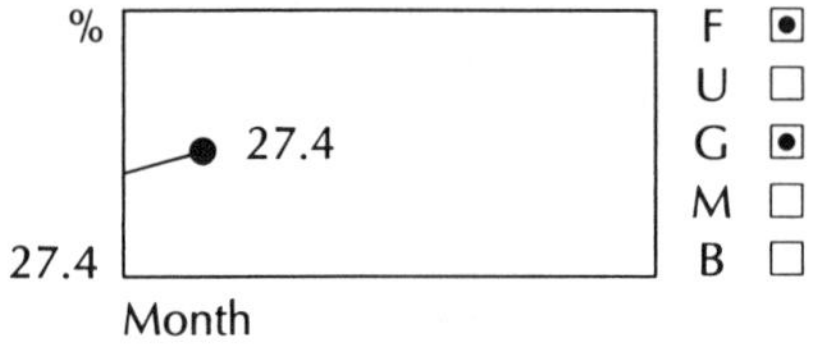

%   ● 27.4   F ▣
                U ☐
                G ▣
27.4   M ☐
Month   B ☐

Figure 36
Trend Graphs—Capital Adequacy and Liquidity Management

Capital Adequacy

Stockholders Equity to
Assets

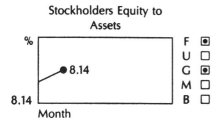

Asset and Liability Management

Interest Rate Sensitivity
(Rate-Sensitive Assets to
Rate-Sensitive Liabilities)

Maturity Matching at
Month-end

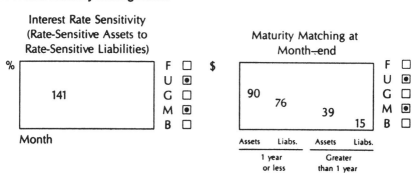

Figure 37
Statement of Income and Expense
(unaudited) ($ in 000)
For the Month of: January 19XX

Financial Highlights	This Month Actual	Last Month Actual	Change from Last Month	F/U	This Month Plan	This Month Variance from Plan	F/U	YTD Actual	YTD Plan	YTD Variance from Plan	F/U
									Year-to-Date (YTD)		
Operating Income											
Interest on Real Estate Loans											
Interest on Non–Real Estate Loans											
Interest on All Securities											
Total Interest Income	1,027.8	1,016.0	11.8	F	1,038.0	–10.2	U	1,027.8	1,038.0	–10.2	U
Less:											
Interest Expense	431.4	430.0	1.4	U	439.0	–7.6	F	431.4	439.0	–7.6	F
Net Interest Income	596.4	586.0	10.4	F	599.0	–2.6	U	596.4	599.0	–2.6	U
Noninterest Income:											
Less: Loss Provisions	58.0	58.0	0		58.0	0	F	58.0	58.0	0	F
Fee Income	47.2	50.0	–2.8	U	47.0	.2	F	47.2	47.0	.2	F
Other Income	8.0	8.0	0	F	8.0	0	F	8.0	8.0	0	F
Total Noninterest Income	55.2	58.0	–2.8	U	55.0	.2	F	55.2	55.0	.2	F
Total Operating Income	593.6	586.0	7.6	F	596.0	–2.4	U	593.6	596.0	–2.4	U
Operating Expense											
Compensation (salaries) & benefits	264.0	280.0	–16.0	F	264.0	0	F	264.0	264.0	0	F
Legal	5.0	0	5.0	F	5.0	0	F	5.0	5.0	0	F

Figure 37 (Continued)

Financial Highlights	This Month Actual	Last Month Actual	Change from Last Month	F/U	This Month Plan	This Month Variance from Plan	F/U	YTD Actual	YTD Plan	YTD Variance from Plan	F/U
Consulting	4.0	4.0	0	F	4.0	0	F	4.0	4.0	0	F
Travel and Entertainment	4.0	5.0	-1.0	F	4.0	0	F	4.0	4.0	0	F
Occupancy	28.0	28.0	0	F	28.0	0	F	28.0	28.0	0	F
Repairs and Maintenance	9.0	9.0	0	F	9.0	0	F	9.0	9.0	0	F
Advertising	12.8	15.0	-2.2	F	12.8	0	F	12.8	12.8	0	F
Stationery and Printing	14.7	15.0	-.3	F	14.7	0	F	14.7	14.7	0	F
Postage and Freight	12.0	12.0	0	F	12.0	0	F	12.0	12.0	0	F
Telephone	10.0	10.0	0	F	10.0	0	F	10.0	10.0	0	F
Data Processing	29.2	31.0	-1.8	F	29.2	0	F	29.2	29.2	0	F
Insurance	4.0	4.0	0	F	4.0	0	F	4.0	4.0	0	F
Audit and Accounting	2.0	2.0	0	F	2.0	0	F	2.0	2.0	0	F
Equipment Rental	36.0	36.0	0	F	36.0	0	F	36.0	36.0	F	F
Depreciation	4.5	4.5	0	F	4.5	0	F	4.5	4.5	0	F
Other	47.1	59.5	-12.4	F	46.8	.3	U	47.1	46.8	.3	U
Other Operating Expenses	222.3	235.0	-12.7	F	222.0	.3	U	222.3	222.0	.3	U
Total Operating Expense	486.3	515.0	-28.7	F	486.0	.3	U	486.3	486.0	.3	U
Earnings—Subsidiaries	2.1	10.1	-8.0	U	5.0	-2.9	U	2.1	5.0	-2.9	U
Operating Income/(Loss) before tax	109.4	81.1	28.3	F	115.0	-5.6	U	109.4	115.0	-5.6	U
Nonoperating Revenue	38.3	0	38.3	F	0	38.3	F	38.3	0	38.3	F
Nonoperating Expense	4.5	0	4.5	U	0	4.5	U	4.5	0	4.5	U
Nonoperating Income	33.8	0	33.8	F	0	33.8	F	33.8	0	33.8	F
Earnings/(Loss) before taxes	143.2	81.1	62.1	F	115.0	28.2	F	143.2	115.0	28.2	F

Figure 38
Consolidated Balance Sheet
for the Month Ended January 19XX

	This Month's Balance	Last Month's Balance	Change from Last Month
Assets			
Earning Assets			
Loans			
Consumer	$29,720.0	$29,000.0	720.0
Real Estate	11,271.3	11,000.0	271.3
Commercial and Industrial	20,653.2	19,820.0	833.2
Interim Construction	17,209.0	18,180.0	−971.0
Total Loans	78,853.5	78,000.0	853.5
Less Loss Reserves	840.6	840.6	0
Net Loans	78,012.9	77,159.4	853.5
Other			
Time Certificates of Deposit	$7,093.0	7,000.0	93.0
Investment Securities	6,784.8	6,341.2	443.6
Federal Funds Sold	23,380.0	23,150.0	230.0
Direct Financing Leases (net)	4,736.2	4,821.3	−85.1
Total Other	41,994.0	41,312.5	681.5
Total Earning Assets	120,006.9	118,471.9	1,535.0
Nonearning Assets			
Cash			
Cash and Noninterest−earning Deposits	$9,161.0	10,085.8	−924.8
Fixed			
Premises and Equipment	5,895.1	5,895.1	0
Real Estate			
Real Estate Held for Sale	6,195.6	6,195.6	0
Other Real Estate Owned	333.3	333.3	0
Other	1,706.2	1,706.2	0
Total Nonearning Assets	$23,291.2	24,216.0	−924.8
Total Assets	$143,298.1	142,687.9	610.2
Liabilities			
Deposits			
Noninterest−bearing Demand	38,034.6	37,793.0	241.6

Figure 38 (Continued)

	This Month's Balance	Last Month's Balance	Change from Last Month
Interest–bearing			
Savings	51,880.1	51,654.7	225.4
Other Time	38,045.6	38,045.6	0
Other Borrowings	1,596.1	1,596.1	0
Total Interest Bearing	91,521.8	91,296.4	225.4
Other			
Other Liabilities	1,520.7	1,520.7	0
Deferred Income Taxes	553.6	496.3	57.3
Commitments and Contingencies	0	0	0
Total Other	2,074.3	2,017.0	57.3
Total Liabilities	131,630.7	131,106.4	524.3
Stockholders' Equity			
Contributed Capital			
Common Stock	9,243.7	9,243.7	0
Retained Earnings	2,423.7	2,337.8	85.9
Total Stockholders' Equity	11,667.4	11,581.5	85.9
Total Liabilities and Stockholders' Equity	143,298.1	142,687.9	610.2

Figure 39
Credit Risk

Loan Quality
For the Month Ended January 19XX

Type of Loan	Good Rating = 1		Moderate Rating = 2		Doubtful Rating = 3		Totals	
	$	R	$	R	$	R	$	R
Consumer	27,700.0		2,020		0		29,720.0	275.0
Real Estate	10,800.0		471.3		0		11,271.3	100.0
Commercial and Industrial	19,524.7		1,128.5		0		20,653.2	370.6
Interim Construction	17,209.0		0		0		17,209	95.0
Total	75,233.7		3,619.8				$78,853.5	$840.6

Good=Loans have been reviewed for quality and no loss reserves have been set aside. One rated.

Moderate=Based on quality review and loss reserves have been set aside. Two rated.

Doubtful=Based on quality review and loss reserves have been set aside for up to 100% of amount at risk. Three rated.

Quarterly Comparison to Peer Group

Every quarter a comparison should be made to one's peer group. This provides a benchmark indicator of areas where your institution may need improvement.

The whole idea of this report is to provide information in lieu of recordkeeping data; performance and risk measures in lieu of nice-to-have information; a facility for communicating control compliance in lieu of supposing; and an active management stance to foster what it takes to become a high-performance institution.

Measuring Performance

Most financial institutions strive to achieve the best performance possible in:

- Profitability

- Loan quality
- Diverse funding
- Service quality

These are the basic ingredients of running a good institution. To perform at the best possible level, an institution must have good planning, be able to measure compliance, have adequate controls, and emphasize quality.

During planning, goals should be set. A set of objectives can be specified for each performance goal. Where they apply, they can be carried down to responsibility centers. More exactness can be attached to them at that level.

Goal	Objectives
• Maximize profitability (increase it by at least 12 percent)	Increase fee income by 15 percent.
	Increase net interest margin by 25 percent.
	Reduce noninterest expenses by 10 percent.
	Reduce staff (FTE) by 10 percent.
• Increase loan quality.	Establish credit rating system.
	Establish incentive program that rewards loan quality instead of quantity.
• Diverse funding.	Increase noninterest bearing deposits by 10 percent.
	Reduce brokered deposits by 15 percent.
• Service quality.	Establish service-level quality objectives for each processing area.

The further down in the organization the more specific the objectives become. The idea is to have a simple and time-effective way to measure compliance and achievement. Below is an example of how those quantifiable objectives are driven down through organization ranks.

Example

Goal and Objectives
Top Level
Maximize Profitability
(Increase it by at least 12 percent)
Major Groups

Line Group A
Business Services
Increase fee income by 15 percent
  Raise fees on business services by 10 percent
  — remittance processing 15 percent
  — collections 5 percent
  — all others 10 percent
Increase business volume by 7 percent

Figure 38 shows how the top-level goals and objectives cascade in the organization. In this example, the top-level goal is to "maximize profitability" through an increase of 12 percent is given specificity as it descends organizationally. Line group A has internalized this goal by listing specific objectives such as to increase fee income by 15 percent.

Once these goals and objectives are known a measurement that tracks them can be established. Some call these key performance indicators or KPIs. KPIs measure a specific performance. The higher up one goes organizationally, the more general the KPIs become. This is consistent with the peel-back philosophy, whereby the further down one goes organizationally the more detailed the information gets. The general KPIs on profitability will measure the budgeted 12 percent increase. Plan-to-actual performance will be measured on this goal in the top management reports. Driving this down to line group A, the goal will be measured on a KPI of how well the objective of a 15 percent increase in fee income is achieved by raising business services fees 10 percent and increasing business volume 7 percent. Units below line group A's management will be measured on specific KPI objectives such as increasing remittance banking fees by 15 percent, collections by 5 percent, all others by 10 percent, and increasing volume by 7 percent.

Today, management is asking its subordinates to answer the following question: "Did you get the job done and achieve the necessary results at the required KPI service level and within cost and other resource constraints?" Getting the job done and achieving the necessary results are related to effectiveness.

KPI service level is related to quality and timeliness. Cost and other resource constraints are related to efficiency.

It is possible to have a highly efficient organization that is ineffective. That is, the organization could be doing a good job but not aligning employee efforts toward achieving goals and objectives related to corporate results. This is why a unified performance reporting system is important. It assures that all departments are concentrating resources on the same corporate goals.

Effectiveness means you are doing the right thing. Efficiency means you are doing it well. The key is to be able to measure both and ensure that they are working together.

Performance Ratios

At a holding company or institution, several performance ratios can be used. What is used depends largely on management style, philosophy, and what is deemed important. Some of the more common measures, which are best used in comparison to one's peer group, are listed as follows:

1. Profitability
   - As a Percentage of Average Total Assets
     —Net interest revenue
     —Noninterest income
     —Noninterest expense
     —Pretax income before securities gains or losses
   - Return on Assets (ROA)
   - Return on Earning Assets (ROEA)
   - Noninterest Income to Noninterest Expense
   - Noninterest Income to Operating Income
   - Service Charges to Deposits
   - Credit Quality
   - As a Percentage of Total Loans
     —Net loan charge-offs
     —Loan loss reserves

- Nonperforming Assets as a Percentage of Total Assets

2. Capital Adequacy
    - Primary Capital as a Percentage of Total Assets
    - Equity Capital as a Percentage of Total Assets
    - Total Capital as a Percentage of Total Assets (Also capital may be measured as a percentage of total liabilities for some institution's capital adequacy.)

3. Productivity
    - Average Total Assets per Employee
    - Net Operating Income per employee
    - Operating Earnings per Employee
    - Personnel Expense per Employee
    - Personnel Expense as a Percentage of Average Total Assets
    - Deposits per Employee
    - Overhead as a Percentage of Operating Income (Non-interest expense to net operating income)
    - Efficiency Ratio

4. Liquidity
    - Loans as a Percentage of Earning Assets
    - Net Purchased Liabilities as a Percentage of Total Assets
    - CDs $100m to Deposits

Risk Measurement

As mentioned earlier, financial institutions face several kinds of risks. Some institutions experience more kinds than others. What kind of risk a financial institution faces depends on its business emphasis. Here's a brief review of basic risks:

1. *Interest-Rate Risk*—The risk that interest rates will change and possibly damage net interest margins and, hence, net interest income.

2. *Liquidity Risk*—The risk that depositors will demand withdrawals beyond availability. The risk of insufficient asset funding.

3. *Capital-Adequacy Risk*—The risk of not having sufficient capital to support assets.

4. *Credit Risk*—The risk that borrowers are either unable or unwilling to pay their debt (loan).

5. *Foreign Exchange Trading*—The risk of an adverse exposure to currency fluctuations.

6. *Operating Risk*—The risk that something didn't get done, wasn't done on time, or done in error.

Several ratios and early warning indicators can show these risks are moving in unfavorable directions. Some risk indicators are listed in the top management report section of this chapter.

Figure 40 shows the risk, measurement ratios, and early warning indicators.

Some of this is elementary but it is intended as a format for identifying risk and early warning indicators. The idea is to be aware of risk and the danger signals that indicate its presence. To manage risk you must set up preventative measures, monitor risk, and take timely corrective action when needed.

Summary

This chapter covered top management reports and measurements of performance and risk. Several tools are available for an executive to keep abreast of performance and risk. An effective executive information and control reporting program can greatly assist an executive in keeping track of the many variables confronting a financial institution.

The emphasis in this book has been on management accounting and how it can help develop solid decision information for executives.

Figure 40
Risk Ratios and Warning Indicators

Risk	Measurement Ratios	Early Warning Indicators
Interest Rate	Spread = Average Earning Asset Yield minus Average Rate on Interest-Bearing Liabilities	Narrowing Spread Lower average yields Higher cost of funds Higher volume of purchased funds Rate sensitivity gap
	Net Interest Margin = Net Interest Income Divided by Average Earnings Assets	Narrowing Interest Margin Lower average yields Higher cost of funds Higher level of nonearning assets Paying above market rates on deposits
Liquidity	Average loans to total deposits	High level of loans to deposits
	$100m and over deposits to assets $100m and over to total deposits	High level of $100m and over deposits
	Brokered deposits	High level of brokered deposits
Capital Adequacy	Equity Capital to Assets Primary Capital to Assets Total Capital to Assets	A decreasing ratio due to asset growth and losses
	Delinquent Loans to Total Capital Nonperforming Loans to Total Capital	Inadequate loss reserves
Credit	Net Losses to Average Loans	Growth in delinquent loans Concentration in country, region, industry Lack of complete documentation Lack of stringent quality rating program Lack of periodic rating review for each loan High level of nonaccrual waivers High level of purchased loan participations Significant number of renegotiated loans Concentration on a few borrowers Lending outside of traditional market area

Figure 40 (Continued)

Risk	Measurement Ratios	Early Warning Indicators
	Loss Reserves to Average Loans	Low loan loss reserves
Foreign Exchange Trading	Net exposure by currency	Large currency exposures
Operating	Service Level Key Performance Indicators Timeliness Efficiency Error Rates	Higher response times, and holdovers Higher processing costs Increased errors

Part III

Issues

8

Funds Transfer Pricing

I n all financial institutions management accounting issues must be resolved constantly. Some serve as a basis for debate. Just about any issue arouses differing views on the solutions. There is no right or wrong answer to many of them. What works for one financial institution may not work for another. Also, the resolution of most management accounting issues centers on philosophy and motivation. The question: "What behavior is management trying to motivate?" leads to most solutions.

Part III will cover the most frequently discussed management accounting issues. They include such high visibility topics as loan loss reserve assignment, equity allocation, funds transfer pricing, the cost of carrying nonperforming loans, overhead reporting, allocation of variances, and shadow accounting. Other topics include foreign exchange variance reporting and prior period adjustment.

What Is Management Accounting?

Management accounting is the process of taking financial accounting and other relevant data and reporting it to management as information for decision making. It is rearranging data, using subjective judgment, and providing focus on relevant information. It is aligning information with management accountability.

To accomplish management accounting requires human intervention, because human judgment and discretion are involved. A great deal of freedom is allowed in practicing management accounting and not particularly constrained by generally accepted accounting principles. Required however, are consistency, accuracy, fairness, and clarity.

Management accounting involves cost analysis; organization, product, and customer profitability reporting; profit planning (budgeting); financial analysis; certain elements of strategic planning; and asset and liability management.

The importance of management accounting is increasing as financial institutions focus on achieving higher performance. Management accounting reflects an institution's philosophy and intended motivation factors. For example, funds transfer pricing is either a motivator or demotivator toward a desired behavior. The setting of a specific rate and pricing structure will motivate behavior in a certain direction. The challenge for those practicing management accounting is to meet the needs of management by setting procedures that motivate intended behavior. Solutions discussed here are considered the most common and practical for industry-wide application.

Of all the management accounting issues today, funds transfer pricing probably is the most frequently discussed. It has tremendous ramifications on unit profitability and performance measurement. But no one methodology seems to please everyone. At best, funds transfer pricing is controversial. If internal rates rise, one group of individuals in the institution (usually funds providers) are pleased. If internal rates fall, another group (usually funds users–lending) applaud.

Conceptual Overview

What is funds transfer pricing (FTP)? Briefly, it is an internal pricing mechanism that charges fund users interest and gives interest revenue credit to fund providers. In some institutions, the system is called funds valuation. It usually is used in determining profitability and motivating staff toward an intended behavior.

The questions to be answered before an FTP system is installed are: What does management want to measure? How does it want to motivate behavior? To be effective, the system must be easy to understand and administer.

Many possible FTP methods are available for a financial institution. They include single-pool concept, multiple-pool concept, matched funding, and contract spreads (see Figure 41). There are variations to each method and the simplest is the single-pool method; next is the more complex multiple-pool method. The most complex method is matched funding.

Single-Pool Method

One example of the single-pool method has the providers and users receiving the same rate. For example, a financial institution has a branch system and it provides $100 in surplus deposits to the head office lending group. Assume the branches receive a 10 percent credit for funds. Then the lending group would pay 10 percent for use of funds. What if the branches' average cost of funds is 8 percent? This would give them a 2 percentage point profit spread. Assume the lending group is pricing its loans at 12 percent. This would also give it a 2 percentage point spread.

For management accounting purposes, we have inflated the institution's interest income and expense by the same amount. Obviously, the percentages cancel out one another. These numbers on an annual basis look like this:

Head Office Lending Group		Branch Group	
$100	Borrowed Funds from the Branches	$100	Surplus Funds
× 10%	Cost of Funds Rate	× 10%	Credit for Funds Rate
$10	Cost of Funds Using	$10	Credit for Funds
		− 8	Cost of Funds at the Branches
		$ 2	Net Before-Tax Profit on Surplus Funds Placed (Provided to Head Office)
$100	Loans		
× 12%	Lending Rate		
$ 12	Interest Revenue		
− 10	Cost of Funds		
$ 2	Net Interest Income		

Impact on Total Financial Institution

$100 Loans

$100   Deposits
$ 12   Interest Revenue
$ 8   Cost of Funds
$ 4   Net Interest Income

If this rate floats with the market, the lending group faces interest-rate risk. This would be contrary to a policy of insulating the group from this risk.

Since this is the simplest method of all, it is the easiest to administer. In this method, one FTP rate is used for charging and crediting funds. The single-pool rate can either represent the institution's effective cost of funds rate or it can represent an outside market rate such as the 90-day Treasury bill (T-bill) rate. Another option is whether FTP should only apply to a branch's or unit's surplus or deficit position, or if all funds should be purchased by the head office pool and sold back. This method is shown in more detail in the following example:

Using the following assumptions the financial institution has:

- Two branches.

- One head office lending unit.

- Branch A is a funds provider (it has $100 in surplus funds).

- Branch B is a funds user (it has $50 in deficit funds).

- Lending unit Z is a funds user (it needs $50 to fund loans).

- A policy of only applying FTP to a net funding position rather than total purchase and sell back.

- A 30-day month.

- Balances that are averages for the month.

- A 365-day year.

In the example at the top of the next page, Branch A is supplying the funds pool with its $100 of surplus. Branch B and Lending Unit Z are using $50 each. They have deficit positions and, therefore, must borrow from the head office pool.

The FTP interest credits and charges are as follows:

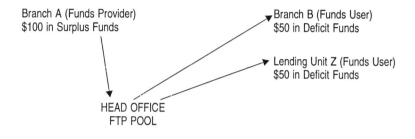

Branch A (Funds Provider)
$100 in Surplus Funds

Branch B (Funds User)
$50 in Deficit Funds

Lending Unit Z (Funds User)
$50 in Deficit Funds

HEAD OFFICE
FTP POOL

Use simple interest formula I = PRT

Where   I   =   Interest
        P   =   Principal
        R   =   Rate
        T   =   Time

Branch A

I = $100 × 8% × 30/365
I = $0.6575 round to $0.66

Branch A receives a $0.66 interest income credit for its surplus funds. This shows up as an income item on the earnings statement.

Branch B

I = $50 × 8% × 30/365
I = $0.3288 round to $0.33

Branch B is charged $0.33 in interest expense for its use of funds.

Lending Unit Z also is charged $0.33 in interest expense.

This means an interest income credit of $0.66 and interest expense charge of $0.66. There were no reconciling items in the FTP system.

Issues

```
                                  $0.33 charge
            $0.66            FTP   ──────────────  Branch B
Branch A  ──────────────
                            Pool  $0.33 charge
                                  ──────────────  Lending Unit Z
```

- Advantages of the single-pool method
  - The single-pool method is simple and easy to understand.
  - It is relatively easy to administer and does not consume large resources.
  - It provides a basic motivation to attract deposits.
  - This method best applies in the following situations:
  - When the financial institution is small.
  - When its funding is relatively stable. For example, when the financial institution has a large core deposit base.
- Disadvantages
  - Depending on FTP basis, users of funds may be subjected to interest-rate risk. (For example, they are subject to rate fluctuations if the 90-day T-bill rate is used as a basis.)
  - If market rates are used as FTP basis, then during high interest rates providers are motivated to attract additional deposits. Users are demotivated because of narrowing spreads (the difference between interest income yield and money costs).
  - This method is not recommended when:
  - The institution is large and has many providers and users.
  - The institution has a relatively volatile funding portfolio—a heavy dependence on purchase funds.

Multiple-Pool Method

The multiple-pool method uses two or more rates in the FTP process. The method is more complex than the single-pool method. Usually it has different rates for providers and users. Also, rates may be stratified by a general maturity pool. Reconciliation of FTP charges and credits becomes more difficult under multiple pool because two or more rates are used.

Assume $100 of funds are provided/used. Also, assume the lending group pays a different rate than the branches receive. Let's say the lending group has to pay 11 percent for the funds it uses and the branches receive 10 percent for the funds they provide. The difference between the two goes into a pool. Some financial institutions create an internal money desk to administer this kind of program. The example follows:

Lending Group		Branches		Internal Funds Money Desk
$100	Borrowed Funds from the Branches	$100	Surplus Funds	
×11%	Cost of Funds Rate	×10%	Credit for Funds Rate	
$ 11	Cost of Funds Used	$ 10	Credit for Funds	$1 Pool Profit

The $1 pool profit does not necessarily reflect the money desk's performance. Let's say the institution's actual average cost of funds is 8 percent. Also, the lending group priced its loan at 12 percent. The institution's overall profitability is calculated as follows:

$12   ($100 × 0.12 = $12)
− 8   ($100 × 0.08 = $ 8)
$ 4   Overall Institution Net Interest Income

Profit Distribution

$1 Lending Group	($12 Revenue less $11 Cost of Funds)
1 Money Pool	($11 Charged to Lending less $10 Paid to Branches)
2 Branches	($10 Received from Money Desk minus $8 Paid to Depositors)
───	
$4 Overall Institution Net Interest Income	

Now take another example of the multiple-pool method with these assumptions:

- One branch is a funds provider. $100 surplus, $80 is long term, $20 is short term.
- One lending unit is a funds user. $100 deficit, $50 is long term, $50 is short term.
- Two pool rates:
  - one each short- and long-term rates for providers 7 percent and 6 percent, respectively.
  - one each short- and long-term rates for users 8 percent and 7 percent, respectively.

  The policy is to only apply FTP to one's net funding position rather than total purchase and sell back.
- Example is for 30-day month.
- Balances are averages for the month.
- 365-day year.

	Example: Overnight Funds	Example: Core Deposits
Branch	Short Term	Long Term
Surplus Funds	$80	$20
	× 0.00575 (1)	× 0.00493 (2)
Credit for Funds	$0.46	$0.10

(1) 7% × 30/365 = 0.00575
(2) 6% × 30/365 = 0.00493

The branch receives $0.56 under the FTP system for their surplus funds.

Now look at the using side of this process.

	Example: 30-day Dealer Flooring	Example: Real Estate Mortgage
Lending Unit	Short-Term Loans	Long-Term Loans
Deficit Funds	$50	$50
(Needed for Loan Funding)	× 0.006575 (1)	× 0.005753 (2)
Charges for Funds		
(Interest Expense)	$0.33	$0.29

(1) 8% × 30/365 = 0.006575
(2) 7% × 30/365 = 0.005753

Here's how the multiple-pool FTP process looks at this point.

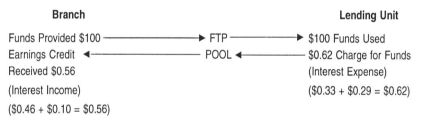

At this point, the FTP pool has a $0.06 profit, they charged the lending unit $0.62, and gave a $0.56 earnings credit.

Differences such as this are not unusual in a multiple-pool FTP system. Also, there was a balance mismatch between short- and long-term funds purchased and short- and long-term funds placed.

Advantages of the multiple-pool method include:

- It provides a closer recognition of market reality by having two rates.

- It provides more rate flexibility than the single-pool method.

Disadvantages of the multiple-pool method are:

- It is sometimes complex and difficult to understand.

- It may result in reconciliation differences.

- It may require more staff and other resources than the single-pool method to administer.

This method works best when:

- A financial institution has several providers and users.
- An institution's balance sheet maturity is mixed between core deposits and purchased funds.

Matched-Funding Method

Matched funding is more sophisticated and complex than the other methods. Under true matched funding, the money desk would go to the money market and purchase funds for new loans. The funding and loans would have the same maturity. The idea is to lock into an interest rate on the funding so the spread or net interest margin (NIM) will be stable through the life of the loan. Hence, the lending unit would be insulated for the most part from interest-rate risk.

In practice, some institutions use a market simulation in the matched-funding method. The FTP pool administrator simulates a matched-funding process and works apart from the money desk in trying to actually match fund loans. However, the administrator does gather information about money market rates and injects them into the FTP system.

In a situation involving matched funding, the institution may or may not simulate matched funding. Its pricing may be based on a money market simulation of matched funding but not actually acquiring matched market funds.

If $100 is being lent to a corporate client for 90 days, the funding desk may decide the 90-day CD rate is appropriate on this transaction. Assume the CD rate is 11 percent. Also, the money desk will quote a customer rate of 13 percent if the lending group uses the guideline that it has to have a 2 percent spread built into the loan. However, the money desk could fund the loan with anything they wanted to. They may have surplus deposits to lend. Say the cost of funds to the money desk is 10 percent. In this deal, there is a 1 percent spread. Some financial institutions use matched funding for large loans. This allows them to back into a known interest spread over the life of the loan.

How does the money desk control profitability? A formula (see Figure 41) assumes the money desk purchases and sells all funds. Here is how a basic formula reads:

1. Interest revenue received on intrainstitution loans,
2. Minus interest expense and brokers' commissions paid for money-market funds,
3. Minus interest revenue received from employee loans,
4. Minus interest expense paid for intrainstitution funds borrowed,
5. Minus average cost of funds rate for institution times capital,
6. Plus average cost of funds rate for institution times employee-loan balances and funding of nonearning assets:
7. Equals assumed controllable contribution to overhead, profit, and taxes.

Here's what each line item of the formula means.

1. Interest revenue received for intrainstitution funds sold represents all of the revenue received by the money desk for internal funds lent. The revenue is what is charged internal funds users.
2. Interest expense and brokers' commissions paid for money-market funds is subtracted from the revenue. The interest represents the cost for funds obtained outside the institution.
3. Employee loan revenue is exchanged from the money desk revenue because it is usually booked at a lower rate than other loans.
4. Interest expense paid for intrainstitution funds purchased is also subtracted from the revenue. The interest represents the cost of funds obtained from providers inside the institution. An example of a provider would be a branch that has surplus funds and places them with the money desk.

Figure 41
Controllable Profitability Formula

(Interest Revenue *for* Intra–Institution Funds Sold)

Minus

(Interest Expense Plus Brokers' Commissions Paid *for* Money Market Funds)

Minus

(Interest Revenue Received from Employee Loans)

Minus

(Interest Expense Paid *for* Intra–Institution Funds Purchased)

Minus

(Average Cost of Funds Rate *for* Institution Times Capital)

Plus

(Average Cost of Funds Rate *for* Institution Times Employee Loan Balances Plus Funding of Nonearning Assets)

=

Assumed Controllable Contribution to Overhead, *and* Profit, *and* Taxes

5. Average cost of funds rate for the institution times capital (equity) is also subtracted from the revenue. The idea is to adjust from the money desk the advantage of having free capital. The average cost of funds rate for the institution excluding capital is multiplied by the institution's capital.

6. Average cost of funds rate for the institution is multiplied by employee loan and nonearning asset balances. The result is added to the balance. The idea is to provide an earnings credit to money desk for funding noncontrollable assets.

7. Assumed controllable contribution to overhead, profit, and taxes is the final result. Nonetheless, other refinements may have to be made to this formula. Sorting out the controllable revenue and expense for the money desk measures its performance.

Using matching simulation, FTP becomes a management accounting process. With actual matched funding, FTP becomes a treasury process. Regardless of FTP, many financial institutions undoubtedly would look to outside incremental funding sources in making extremely large loans.

Let's take a detailed example with the following assumptions:

- Simulated match funding.
- Two branches.
- Branch A is a funds provider. $100 surplus ($70 is long term, $20 is medium term, and $10 is short term).

  (Breakdown is derived using their funding mix as a proxy.)
- Branch B is a funds user. It has an overnight funding need of $10.
- One corporate lending unit is lending $25 for three months.
- The pool rates for providers are:
  - Long term 6 percent
  - Medium term 6.5 percent
  - Short term 7 percent

Issues

- The overnight funding rate is 7.25 percent.
- The 90-day CD (market rate) is 6.75 percent.
- Only net surplus funds are purchased from providers.
- Example is for 30-day month.
- Balances are averages for the month.
- 365-day year.

What we have here is a combination of the multiple-pool method and matched funding. The multiple-pool method is used here to give earnings credits to providers. Matched funding is employed to charge the users of the funds. At this point, it must be mentioned, there are several variations to FTP methods. The following is a basic, practical approach:

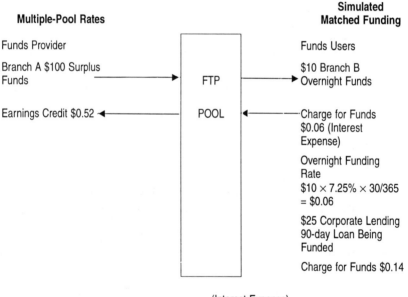

Multiple-Pool Rates

Simulated Matched Funding

Funds Provider

Branch A $100 Surplus Funds

FTP

Funds Users

$10 Branch B Overnight Funds

Earnings Credit $0.52

POOL

Charge for Funds $0.06 (Interest Expense)

Overnight Funding Rate
$10 × 7.25% × 30/365 = $0.06

$25 Corporate Lending 90-day Loan Being Funded

Charge for Funds $0.14

(Interest Expense)
90-day CD rate
$25 × 6.75% × 30/365 = $0.14

Long Term $70 × 6% × 30/365 = $0.35
Medium Term $20 × 6.5% × 30/365 = $0.11
Short Term $10 × 7% × 30/365 = $0.06
Total $0.52

At this point, it would be difficult to reconcile all the items. The FTP matched-funding method is a fluid process. That is, it will not balance between funding credits and charges. Also, there probably will be a funding profit or loss in the FTP pool.

Advantages of the matched-funding method are:

- It parallels market rates and is more exacting.

- It provides interest rate stability by locking in a known cost of funds.

- It provides more flexibility than single- or multiple-pool methods.

Disadvantages of the matched-funding method include:

- It is complex and difficult to understand.

- It will result in reconciling differences.

- The FTP pool becomes a pseudo-profit center if the simulated method is used.

- It requires more resources to administer than the single- and multiple-pool methods.

This method works best when:

- An institution has several providers and users.

- An institution's balance sheet maturity is mixed.

- An institution has extensive resources (human and computer) available.

- An institution wishes to insulate its lending units from interest-rate risk.

Contract-Spread Method

The last FTP method to discuss is the contract spread. This FTP method is most commonly used when funding international loans. When booking a loan, lending officers get a quote on a spread from the money desk. The spread is expressed in basis points: 100

basis points being 1.0 percent. The spread is the difference between yield and cost of funds. In using this method, the money desk assumes all interest-rate risk. Nonetheless, the lending unit has to conform to pricing guidelines to realize the spread.

The multiple-pool FTP method can run parallel to this method. Multiple pool will only handle surplus funds and deficits in aggregate from each location or unit. It will not address individual loans. So it's possible to have a multiple-pool FTP and contract spreads working at the same time. The funds are mutually exclusive, however.

Here's an example of funding a $100 loan. The pricing guidelines are 10.25 percent. The money desk quotes a spread of 225 basis points or 2.25 percent. This means the guaranteed funding rate is 8 percent ($10.25 - 2.25 = 8.0$).

The net interest income for a 30-day month will be $0.18 ($100 $\times$ 2.25% $\times$ 30/365 = $0.18).

This spread can be booked into the loan funding system so the net interest income for the loan is calculated monthly.

Advantages of the contract-spread funding method are:

- It insulates lending units from interest-rate risk.

- It provides preciseness on individual loan NIM.

- It provides another dimension of flexibility in FTP.

The one major disadvantage is that it requires an extensive tracking mechanism and human resources.

This method can be applied in at least two ways:

- To international lending.

- To wholesale lending by domestic financial institutions.

The method's success depends on the funding unit's ability to adequately protect the institution from interest-rate risk.

Summary

A financial institution's philosophy, information systems, and organization structure are some of the factors that determine where the FTP method will fit best.

Behavioral implications exist in each FTP method and management must understand what kinds of behavior will be motivated in selecting a particular method.

There isn't any particularly right or wrong FTP method discussed in this chapter. That's because management accounting is mostly for internal management use to measure performance based on the financial institution's philosophy. The right method for a financial institution is one that motivates behavior according to management's wishes and measures performance based on its philosophy.

Some methods make more sense than others. Also, some are more popular. The decision on which method to use should coincide with the institution's culture and philosophy.

Figure 42
Funds Transfer Pricing (FTP) Methods

Method	How It Works	Advantages	Disadvantages	Application
Single Pool (SP)	One rate for provider and user. Could be internal COF or external market rate. Lending unit absorbs interest-rate risk.	Simple and easy to understand. Relatively easy to administer. Provides basic motivation to attract deposits.	Rate fluctuations will cause earnings instability. Users are subjected to interest-rate risk.	Small financial institutions. Stable portfolio (e.g., large core deposit base).
Multiple Pool (MP)	Two or more rates. Could have different rates for provider and user. Also can stratify rates by maturity. Could use internal COF on market rates. Lending unit largely absorbs interest-rate risk.	Closer to market reality. Provides more flexibility.	Sometimes complex and difficult to understand. May result in reconciling differences. Requires more resources to administer.	Used in institutions that have several providers and users. Mixed portfolio (mixed maturity and interest rates).
Matched Funding (MF)	Fund users are charged based on market rates. Tied to loan maturity. FTP system is usually a hybrid of MP and MF.	Market reality. Insulates users from interest-rate risk.	Complex. Requires resources to administer. Difficult to reconcile differences.	Used mostly to fund loans. Used when institution has extensive computer system and resources. Used in larger institutions.
Contract Spreads (CS)	Loans are funded with money desk quotes on contract spreads. Works in tandem with organizational FTP.	Market reality. Insulates users from interest-rate risk.	Requires extensive tracking system.	Applies to international lending. Also domestic wholesale. Product funding as contrasted to FTP for organizational funding.

9

Allocation Issues

Each issue in this chapter has a variety of resolutions. As mentioned before, there isn't only one way to resolve the issues. Therefore, the most common approach to each issue is discussed. Alternative methods also are explored where appropriate.

Allocating Loan Losses, Reserves, and Provisions

This issue asks whether a financial institution should allocate loan loss reserves and subsequent provisions, charge losses to lending units, retain losses in a corporate pool, or employ a combination of the latter two. When an institution allocates either loan loss reserves and provisions or levies assessments for write-offs (see Figure 44) to lending units, it essentially is aligning authority with responsibility. This issue is important because it affects the reported profitability performance of a lending unit. The possible alternatives include:

1. Allocate loan loss reserves to lending units based on portfolio quality and update monthly with provisions, but don't assess them for charge-offs. Report charge-offs as a memo item.

2. Initially allocate loss reserves to lending units and update monthly with provisions, but also assess them for charge-offs.

3. Only allocate loan losses (charge-offs) to lending units as they occur.

4. Retain loan loss reserves (and, hence, provisions) and charge-offs on a corporate level.

Let's take each possibility and explore its advantages and disadvantages and also look at variations of each possibility:

1. Allocate loan loss reserves to lending units based on portfolio quality and update monthly with provisions, but don't assess them for charge-offs. Report charge-offs as a memo item.

Under this method, the underlying philosophy is that the lending units are accountable for deterioration in loan quality but should not be assessed for charge-offs. Therefore, loss reserves are assigned initially based on portfolio quality. The reserves are updated monthly with increased provisions being charged as an expense to the lending unit.

The advantages of this method are: Authority for lending and responsibility for loan quality are aligned closely; the institution has a proxy for determining the adequacy of loss reserves; and this heightens awareness of the need for loan quality throughout the institution.

A disadvantage of this method is that the accountability for charge-offs is assigned to a corporate pool. This drawback is shored up in method 2. The initial provision is established as follows:

*   Develop a numerical credit-rating system for your commercial loan portfolio.

    For example, a rating of 1 to 9; 1 is the highest quality possible and 9 is a charge-off. Loss factors should be developed for commercial loans by category, industry, and country. The loss factors can be developed by analyzing the bank's loss experience and also by compiling information on industry-loss experience.

Develop loss factors by category (loan type) for any consumer loans your bank may have.

An example of a loan type is direct auto loans. A test can be run by simulating an assignment of these factors to each lending unit's portfolio. Check the resulting aggregate indicated loss reserve against the institution's present aggregate reserve.

Once satisfied that your factors are viable and in line with the institution's loss reserves, begin assigning them to all lending units based on their loan portfolios. First, allocate reserves to special situations such as the loan work-out portfolio based on a probability of charge-offs. Then allocate the rest to the portfolio based on the percent of remaining reserves.

At this point, you must understand what the general ledger accounting entry is when additional loss reserves are put on the books as in the following:

	Debit	Credit
Loan Loss (Provisions)	Expense	
Loan Loss (Reserves)		Retained Earnings

When the institution actually incurs a loss the following general ledger entry is made:

	Debit	Credit
Loan Loss (Reserves)	Retained Earnings	
X Y Z Loan		Asset-Loans

Figure 43 shows how the loss-reserve method works.

This example is for an entire institution. The loan categories are sorted according to commercial loans and consumer loans. Each has subcategories. There is also a line for unassigned corporate reserves. Write-offs are listed on a memo basis. As discussed previously, the loss factors for each loan category, rating, and type are listed under the "loss factor" column.

These factors can be developed through your institution's industry experience. They can be refined further by analyzing the industry to which you are lending and the geographic implications of your borrowers. Loan balances outstanding are listed under the "loan balances outstanding" column. The column 4 "indicated reserve" is the result of multiplying column 2 "loss factor" by column 3 "loan balances outstanding." It indicates what the institu-

195

Figure 43
Loss Reserve Method Example

(Col. 1) Loan Category	(Col. 2) Loss Factor	(Col. 3) Loan Balances Outstanding	(Col. 4) Indicated Reserve	(Col. 5) Last Month's Remaining Reserve (Net Reserves)	(Col. 6) Current Month Provision* Surplus/ (Deficit)	(Col. 7) Nonperforming Balances
Commercial Loans						
Rating 1	0.0050	950	4.7500	4.7500	0	0
2	0.0060	120	0.7200	0.7200	0	0
3	0.0075	115	0.8625	0.8625	0	0
4	0.0100	143	1.4300	1.4300	0	0
5	0.0160	15	0.0240	0.0240	0	0
6	0.2500	30	7.5000	7.5000	0	0
7	0.3500	20	7.0000	7.0000	0	0
8	0.8000	75	60.0000	50.0000	(10)	75
Total		$1,468	82.2865	72.2865	(10)	75
Consumer Loans						
Direct Auto	0.016	10	0.1600	0.1600	0	0
Indirect Auto	0.017	7	0.1190	0.1190	0	0
Conventional Mortgages	0.005	15	0.0750	0.0750	0	0
		$32	0.3540	0.3540	0	0

* Column 5 minus Column 4 = Column 6.

Figure 43 (Continued)

(Col. 1) Loan Category	(Col. 2) Loss Factor	(Col. 3) Loan Balances Outstanding	(Col. 4) Indicated Reserve	(Col. 5) Last Month's Remaining Reserve (Net Reserves)	(Col. 6) Current Month Provision* Surplus/ (Deficit)	(Col. 7) Nonperforming Balances
Beginning Unassigned Corporate Reserves				15.0000	15	—
Net Unassigned Corporate Reserves Total		$1,500	82.6405	87.6405	5	75
Memo write-offs $20.						

* Column 5 minus Column 4 = Column 6.

tion's reserves should be based on factors derived and the balances outstanding in each category, rating, and type. Column 5 is the preceding month's remaining reserves. It is possible for reserves to change during the month if loans are transferred to the work-out group. Column 6 is the indicated provision surplus or deficit as indicated by ( ). It is the result of subtracting column 4 from column 5. This example shows that the institution has a provision deficit of $10 for No. 8 loans. The institution can either take out a new provision that would impact its income statement as an expense or take the $10 out of the unassigned corporate reserves. There is $15 in unassigned corporate reserves. If the $10 were taken from the pool, $5 would be left in unassigned reserves. This method allows the institution to check the adequacy of its reserves monthly. Under this method of calculating reserve adequacy, a great deal of reliance is placed on the validity of the loss factors. Column 7 reports the "nonperforming balances."

In this example, an "8" rating indicates a nonperforming loan and this "8" rated commercial loan has a loss factor of 0.8 assigned to it. This means there is an 80 percent probability of a charge-off. Usually nonperforming loans are transferred to a work-out group. If this were a lending unit's report, its nonperforming loans probably would not remain on the unit's report as the loans would be sold to the work-out group at a discount. The indicated discount here is $0.80 on the dollar. That is, the work-out group would only have to pay $0.20 on the dollar ($1.00 − $0.80 = $0.20) for "8" rated nonperforming loans.

Now, apply this method to a commercial lending unit.

Under this method, you won't necessarily have to reduce the loss provision for the unit when balances drop. However, you would increase the provision in all cases of indicated deficits. Figure 44 is an example of how this would work for lending unit A.

In this example, there is a loss reserve surplus of $0.75 in the "7" rated loans. This could be caused by a reduction in loan balances such as a loan payoff. The surplus could be sold back to the institution's unassigned loss reserve pool and, thereby, favorably affect unit A's income statement for the month being reported. Or the surplus could be held in the unit's reserve for future use.

Figure 44
Loss Reserve Method Applied to Commercial Loans

Loan Category	Loss Factor	×	Loan Balances Outstanding	=	Indicated Reserve	Last Month's Reserve	Current Month Provision Surplus/(Deficit)	Nonperforming Balances
Commercial Loans								
Rating								
1	0.0050		10		0.050	0.050		
2	0.0060		25		0.150	0.150		
3	0.0075		30		0.225	0.225		
4	0.0100		50		0.500	0.500		
5	0.0160		15		0.240	0.240		
6	0.2500		5		1.250	1.250		
7	0.3500		15		5.250	6.000	0.75	
8	0.0800		0		0	0	0	
			$150		7.665	8.415	0.75	0

Memo write-offs $1.

Unit A also experienced a $1.00 write-off. The report shows it as a memo item.

Here's a recap of the methodology for this alternative:

- Use credit ratings for larger loans (commercial) to establish provision. Develop factors based on your institution's and the financial services industry's loss experience.

- Use your institution's and the financial services industry's experience by category (loan type) for consumer loans (for example, direct-auto loans).

- Check overall reasonableness of reserves by aggregating total, calculating percent to total loans, and comparing against total institution and industry average.

The whole process of allocating loan loss reserves to profit centers could be administered as follows:

- Develop loss factors for commercial loans by credit rating, using your institution and financial services industry experience as a basis.

- Develop loss factors for consumer loans by type, using your institution and financial services industry experience as a basis.

- Apply these factors to the institution's loan portfolio and again test the overall reserves for reasonableness. Make adjustments as necessary.

- Assign initial reserves to each lending unit based on these factors. No income statement impact would occur for this initial allocation.

- Reconcile allocated reserves to total institution reserves. The difference would be "unassigned loss reserves" and would be held at the corporate level.

- Apply the factors (constants) each month to the loan balances outstanding (variables) to arrive at an indicated reserve for each category held by a given lending unit. Periodically—at least once a year—update the factors.

- Compare the indicated reserves to the preceding month's remaining reserves. Surpluses could be sold back to the corporate unassigned-loss-reserves pool. Deficits would create a need to allocate a provision in the current month. This would have an income statement impact for the lending unit affected. For example, when a loan is taken off a lending unit's books, the reserve could be sold to the unassigned pool.

- The reserve factor for nonperforming commercial loans serves as a proxy for discounting those loans to the work-out group. For example, if the loss factor for 8 rated loans is 0.8, they are in effect sold at $0.20 on the dollar ($1.00–$0.80=$0.20) when they are conveyed to the work-out group. The lending unit absorbs the $0.80 loss. In conjunction with this, a policy could be implemented for the work-out group to cover the cost of carry for loans it purchases from the lending units. If the group buys a loan at $0.20 on the dollar and is able to recover more, this serves as an internal profit incentive for it.

- Write-offs are reported only on a memorandum.

A lending unit's income statement could be formatted as follows:

Revenue

Net Interest Income	$10
Fee Income	2
Other Income	1

Expenses

Operating Expense	7
Loss Provisions Expense/(Credit)	1*
Net Profit before Tax	$5

---

* The total of all allocations of provisions and reserves should tie to or reconcile with the institution's total listed in the general ledger.

The loss provision could either be an expense to cover deficits or a credit to indicate reserves sold back to the unassigned corporate reserves pool.

This method is time-consuming and may require more resources than an institution is willing to devote. A much simpler approach is to develop an overall factor and assign it to each unit's loan balances regardless of ratings and loan types. First, subtract any loan balances and associated loss reserves for nonperforming loans assigned to the work-out group. The probability for loss then can be estimated for each major loan.

For example:

	Loss Reserves	Outstanding Loans
Total Institution	$87.6405	$1,500.00
Direct Assignment to Work-out Department	−50.0000	−75.00
Net Balances	$37.6405	$1,425.00

Then calculate an overall reserve ratio for the institution and assign this factor to each lending unit as their initial loss provision allocation.

Ratio Calculation Formula:
Loan Loss Reserves ÷ Loan Balances = Loss Reserve Factor
Loan Loss Reserves $37.6405 ÷ Loan Balances
$1,425 = Loss Reserve Factor 2.64%

Loan loss reserves are therefore assigned on a gross basis to all lending units at 2.64 percent of their loan balances. For example: Lending unit A has $150 in loans. Therefore, $150 × 2.64% = $3.96 allocated loss reserves to lending unit A.

In looking back at the first example for unit A using specific factors, a significant difference is seen between the allocation of reserves based on specific categories, ratings, and types—$7.665, and the broad approach of 2.64 percent of performing loan balances—$3.96. Although these are examples, they point out one of the possible disadvantages of a broad approach to allocating reserves. In allocating on a broad basis you lose perspective on specific loan quality and, hence, risk.

In the example of the broad approach, management accounting would maintain the loss reserve ratio for each lending unit at 2.64 percent of performing loans outstanding. For example:

	Performing Loans Outstanding	Loss Reserve Factor	Indicated Loss Reserve	Current Month Provision
Month 1	150 ×	0.0264 =	3.960	
Month 2	155 ×	0.0264 =	4.092	*0.132

*(4.092–3.960=0.132)

Assume in this same month that $10 in nonperforming loans were transferred to the work-out group and, therefore, do not appear on this chart. This means that $15 in new loans were put on the books ($150 – $10 + $15 = $155).

Let's look at the next alternative:

2. Initially allocate loss reserves and charge the lending units for write-offs. Under this alternative, a lending unit would sell its reserves back to the unassigned corporate pool when it transfers loans to the work-out group. However, the unit would receive a charge on its income statement for losses (charge-offs) incurred. Also, the unit would receive a credit for recoveries received. Who is to bear the cost of carry (cost of funding) on nonperforming loans and the administrative cost of the work-out group would have to be determined. It is a separate issue. If such costs were charged to the lending units their income statement would appear as follows:

Revenue

Net Interest Income	$15
Fee Income	2
Other Income	1
Total Revenue	18

Expenses

Operating Expenses	$10
Loss Provision Expense/(Credit)	2
Nonperforming Loan Expenses	3
Charge-offs	2

Total Expenses	17
Net Profit before Tax	$ 1

Next is alternative 3. Only allocate loan losses (charge-offs) to lending units as they occur.

Under this method you would not allocate loss reserves to the lending units. However, you would charge them for loan losses as they occur. Their income statement would appear as follows:

Revenue

Net Interest Income	$15
Fee Income	2
Other Income	1
Total Revenue	18

Expenses

Operating Expenses	10
Charge-offs	2
Total Expense	12
Net Profit Before Tax	$ 6

This method tends to cause wide fluctuations in a lending unit's earnings trend. There is no gradual build up of reserves to smooth out the impact of charge-offs. Also, another disadvantage of this method is the lead/lag effect of bad loans. Lending officers responsible for the loans may no longer be in the unit that is accountable for a charge-off.

This brings us to alternative 4. Retain loan loss reserves and write-offs on a corporate level.

Revenue

Net Interest Income	$15
Fee Income	2
Other Income	1
Total Revenue	18

Expenses

Operating Expenses	10
Total Expense	10
Net Profit before Tax	$ 8

In situations where reserves and subsequent provisions are allocated, they must tie to or reconcile with the institution's total.

Allocating the Cost of Carry (Cost of Capital) for Nonearning Assets

This issue has three subsets. They ask (1) should the institution's property and equipment be assigned to individual responsibility centers (RCs)? (2) should a cost of carry be applied to the institution's property and equipment? and (3) if each lending unit's non-performing loans aren't sold out or transferred to the workout group, should the units be charged for the cost of carry for these loans?

1. Should the institution's property and equipment be assigned to individual responsibility centers (RCs)? In management accounting, the more detail used in tracking and calculating, the more time the staff will need to administer the program. Keep this in mind when considering a management accounting enhancement. However, there is merit in tracking. It can help a manager keep tabs on equipment. Also, depreciation can be readily identified with an RC and, thereby, provide a more complete financial picture. This is especially useful at centers where expensive machinery and mainframe computers are in use. Such tracking assist those conducting cost studies.

   Some equipment is best accounted for on a pool basis. For example, furniture and computer terminals can be placed in cost pools and charged out on some unit basis to responsibility centers (RCs). Furniture expense could be charged to RCs on a head count basis, and computer terminals on per terminal use.

   Allocating real property such as land and buildings to a responsibility center, such as a branch, may create a disproportionate burden or benefit to the branch. For example, assume a branch is on a fully depreciated property. If assigned this property, the branch would only have to

Figure 45
Allocation of Loan Losses and Reserves

Impact/Implications	Do Not Allocate Reserves and Write-offs	Allocate Reserves Only	Allocate Write-Offs Only	Allocate Both Reserves and Memo Write-Offs
Earnings Implications	Does not reflect true profitability.	Reflects financial accounting. Tends to smooth out loss effect.	Causes wide swings in earnings. Difficult to budget and control.	Recognizes financial accounting. Provides visibility on charge-offs.
Management Philosophy	Loan losses are a corporate issue only. Don't want to devote resources to allocations.	Losses should be amortized instead of direct charges that cause fluctuations in earnings. Motivates lending officers toward loan quality. Memo reporting of charge-offs is not necessary.	Losses should be recognized as they occur. Motivates lending officers toward loan quality.	Losses should be amortized instead of direct charges that cause fluctuations in earnings. Motivates lending officers toward loan quality.
Maintenance and System Impact	None	Requires staff and computer resources for quarterly maintenance.	Requires staff and computer resources for quarterly maintenance.	Requires staff and computer resources for quarterly maintenance.
Profitability Reporting Organizational Impact	None	Adjusts earnings.	Adjusts earnings.	Adjusts earnings.
Product Impact	Will not reconcile to org. reporting.	Will reconcile to org. reporting.	Will not reconcile to org. reporting.	Will reconcile to org. reporting.
Customer Impact	None	None	None	None

pay taxes, maintenance, and utilities. It would not have to absorb depreciation.

In institutions where a central property management department controls all properties and retains the asset on central books, branch asset administration and reporting is easier. Under this arrangement, the property management department could create rent pools and charge each RC rent based on square footage and prevailing rates in its geographic location.

Some would appropriately argue that the real cost of the branch as a location should be known when deciding on continuing and closing RCs. When this occurs data would be available from the central property management department.

2. Should a cost of carry be applied to the institution's property and equipment? Take a branch that has new facilities. If it were assigned the book value of the property on the general ledger the branch would have to fund it. Also, it is a nonearning asset. This would create a need for additional funds to service the asset. If the branch provides funds then it implicitly has absorbed the cost of carry. If it is a fund user, that is, it has to borrow from head office, it explicitly is paying the cost of carry, assuming a funds transfer pricing mechanism is used. This method has it merits but can be costly to maintain.

Consider a data processing center that has considerable equipment. Assume its equipment has a book value of $3.6 million. It would receive a depreciation charge of $100,000 a month. If a cost of carry is added to this, the center would be charged the $100,000 depreciation plus the cost of carrying book value of the equipment.

3. If each lending unit's nonperforming loans are not sold out or transferred to a work-out group, should those units be charged for the cost of carry for these loans?

In some institutions, nonperforming loans are transferred to the work-out group at book value, and the work-out group assumes carrying costs for those loans. If management's intent is to align responsibility of bad loans with lending authority, such costs should be assigned to the lending units originating the loans. This provides more clarity of organizational profitability. This has a drawback in that some lending managers may refute the loans and claim they were not in authority when the loans were made. This objection could be handled by reporting the costs as a memo item.

Another drawback is the time the staff takes to assign costs of carry. On the plus side, assigning the cost of carry serves to elevate cost consciousness.

Allocating Equity (Capital)

In trying to measure return on equity (ROE), some institutions allocate equity to their profit centers. The main reasons financial institutions allocate capital are:

1. To facilitate a return on equity measurement. A popular trend in performance measurement is to measure profit centers by their return on equity (ROE). To do so, profit centers must be allocated equity. The formula for a total institution's return on equity is:

Leverage $\times$ Return on Assets (ROA) = Return on Equity (ROE)

Where Leverage = Average Total Assets $\div$ Average Shareholder Equity

Where ROA = Income Before Securities Transactions $\div$ Average Total Assets

For purposes of measuring a profit center's ROE, use this formula:

$$\frac{\text{Net Profit after Tax (YTD)} \div \text{(Months YTD)} \times (12)}{\text{Equity Allocated to Profit Center (YTD Average)}}$$

As you can see, equity must be allocated to asset-based profit centers to measure their ROE. A numerical example is presented later.

2. To recognize the finite resource of capital as it pertains to business entities within the institution. The thought here is that capital is a finite resource. An institution has only a

certain amount of capital. Therefore, it must be certain that capital being deployed will realize a reasonable return. By allocating capital to profit centers, management is better able to make astute decisions on business ventures, including its type of lending.

Reasons for not allocating equity are:

1. An institution may not want to measure ROE of profit centers because resource requirements are too high for reporting or because it doesn't believe in its value. This is a basic philosophic issue. Some institutions see ROE as an important measurement but can't see it as a helpful or valid profit center measure.

2. An institution's management doesn't want to spend resources necessary to administer an equity allocation system. Management may see it as too expensive to administer.

3. An institution's management wants to keep reporting simplified. It may believe that equity allocation and ROE is an unnecessary embellishment on performance reports. Equity allocation may be viewed as cluttering reports and wasting management time in resolving possible dissent.

Factors to Consider

Several factors must be considered in setting up and administering an equity allocation system.

1. It requires staff resources to administer. Much time is consumed to research and set up an equity allocation system. Profitability report formats will have to be modified to include equity allocation. For example:

    A basis for allocation must be decided. Several bases can be used. One is the regulatory net worth to assets requirement as a proxy for allocating equity. For example, if the regulatory weighted average net worth requirement is 7.5 percent of assets, then equity would be allocated to asset-based profit centers using this percentage. This is the most popular method because it is relatively easy to administer and understand.

Some financial institutions use a complex scheme in which each asset category is allocated a different percentage based on that asset's risk. (They simulate regulatory allocating of capital as a percentage of risk-weighted assets.) Hence, capital is allocated based on asset balances and their relative risk. This method also is time-consuming to administer.

2. Decide who to allocate to. The possibilities include: allocating to asset-based profit centers, fee-based profit centers, and cost centers. If equity is allocated to fee-based centers, a method must be devised on how to allocate equity, because normally there are no assets. This would serve to provide a highly artificial ROE measurement. More on this later.

   If equity is allocated to cost centers, it would eventually have to be reallocated to profit centers, because ROE cannot be measured when there is no income.

3. Revise funds transfer pricing (funds valuation) methodology to accommodate allocations. If there is a fund valuation attached to equity allocations, it will affect the funds transfer pricing (FTP) methodology. The two must complement one another. For example, allocate $75 equity to lending unit A. Also, give it interest credit for the funds. It has $1,000 in loans outstanding. Where previously it needed to borrow $1,000 from the money desk, now it only needs to borrow $925 ($1,000 – $75.00). Also, instead of paying interest on $1,000, unit A is only paying interest on $925. Besides, it is receiving interest credit for $75. The differences on the cost of funds and its effect on FTP are contrasted as follows:

FTP without Equity Allocation		FTP Impact with Equity Allocation	
$1,000	Needed to Fund Loans	$925.00	Needed to Fund Loans
× 8%	Annual Interest Rate	× 8%	Annual Interest Rate
$ 80	Annual Cost of Funds for Unit A	$74.00	Annual Cost of Funds (COF)
		$75.00	Equity Allocation
	The $80 is Credited to	× 8%	Credit for Funds
	the FTP Pool Income	$ 6.00	Annual Credit for Funds
		$74.00	Annual COF
		– 6.00	Credit
		$68.00	Net COF

Unit A has the necessary $1,000 to fund loans. But it only has to pay on $925 of the funding. The free $75 equity allocation provides the unit with a reduction in interest expense.

This method is probably the most used of the two that provide an interest expense reduction to the recipient organization. Assuming equal rates, it has the same effect as giving equity free, buying it back for pool use, and then selling it back to the unit.

4. Evaluate interest. In allocating equity, an institution has the following choices: (1) allocate equity as free capital, (2) charge interest for equity allocated, (3) give interest credit for equity allocated, or (4) allocate equity as a memo item only.

    The prevalent method of valuation is to give interest credit, either explicit or implicit, for equity allocated. Method 1 provides explicit credit, and Method 2 provides implicit credit.

Let's take each method and discuss it in more detail.

1. Allocate equity as free capital. Under this method, the recipient unit essentially is receiving an implicit interest

credit, because it is receiving capital and doesn't have to pay interest on the money. Continuing with the previous example of unit A, assume the following:

Unit A previously had to pay $80 for its $1,000 funding needs. Now the funding costs are only $74.00.

$925.00	Remaining Needed to Fund Loans
× 8%	Annual Interest Rate
$ 74.00	Annual Cost to Fund Loans
$ 75.00	Free Equity

2. Charge interest for equity allocated. Under this method, the amount of equity allocated would be a substitute for funds provided to the recipient unit. But it would still have to pay for it.

In an example of how this would work, assume the same rate is applied to transfer pool funds and equity as follows:

$ 925.00	Funds from Transfer Pool
$ 75.00	Equity
$1,000.00	Amount to Fund Loans
× 8%	
$ 80	Annual Cost to Fund Loans

As you can see, this method impacts the FTP system. It does so because pricing is applied not only to the funding pool but also to equity. This suggests an adjustment would have to be made in pricing funds, because equity is a noninterest cost source of funds to the institution.

The method has merits in that recipient units are not only being measured by equity but have to pay for it as a resource. Some financial institutions charge subsidiaries for capital as though it were a loan.

In this example, unit A paid $80 via the FTP system before equity allocation. With equity allocation, unit A receives a $6.00 credit for the equity allocated to it plus it has free use of funds.

Unit A's net cost of funds is now $68.00. If the FTP system previously had used equity as part of its funding, it would have to be adjusted both for funding and pricing.

3. Give interest credit for equity allocated. This method has the lowest cost of funds possible for lending unit A as the following shows:

$925.00	Remaining Needed to Fund Loans
× 8%	Annual Interest Rate
$ 74.00	Annual Cost to Fund Loans
$ 75.00	Equity
× 8%	Credit for Funds Interest Rate
$ 6.00	Credit for Equity

Unit A's funding is as follows:

		Cost/(Credit)	
$ 925.00	Pool	$74.00	
$ 75.00	Equity	($ 6.00)	
$1,000.00	Total	$68.00	Net Cost of funds

In this example, lending unit A is not only receiving $75 equity but it also is getting credit for it, essentially a double benefit. Unit A has free use of the $75 and also receives an interest credit for it.

However, this method has its drawbacks because it lowers a recipient's cost of funds below what is prudent and practical. That is, it fails to simulate marketplace reality. Therefore, the recipient's interest margins could be higher than normal and, hence, distort the measurement of performance.

4. Allocate equity only as a memo item. Under this method, FTP is not impacted because equity is not considered part of the lending unit's funding. The example below shows the funding needs are $1,000.

$1,000	Needed to Fund Loans
× 8%	Annual Interest Rate
$ 80	Annual Cost to Fund Loans
Memo:	$75 Equity

Since equity is memo allocated, it is not used for funding. It is used only for a return on equity (ROE) measurement. Under methods, 1, 2, and 3, equity serves a dual purpose: It is used for funding and ROE measurement. Under method 4, it is used only for an ROE measurement.

- Interest Rates

The selection of an interest rate depends on how one wants to affect the FTP mechanism. In the examples presented here, the FTP pool rate was used arbitrarily to calculate interest for FTP pool funds and equity. This is not necessary. However, whatever interest rate is used for equity should be calculated against balances and tested for reconciliation or compatibility with the FTP mechanism.

- Allocation Bases

Three basic possibilities to be discussed here include: (1) allocate equity based on financial institution's regulatory-required weighted average ratio of capital to assets, (2) allocate equity based on financial institution's actual ratio of capital to assets, or (3) allocate equity based on individually identified risk-based assets.

1. Allocate equity based on weighted average regulatory-required ratio of capital to assets.

     For example, assume that the weighted average regulatory requirement is 7.5 percent. Also, assume the institution has $200 in capital and $2,900 in assets. There are two lending units. Unit A is domestic and has $1,000 in loans; unit B is international and has $700 in loans. The capital is allocated as follows:

	Unit A	Unit B
*Loans	$1,000	$700
Regulatory Capital Percent Requirement	× 7.5%	× 7.5%
	$ 75	$52.50

Thus, $75 is allocated to unit A, and $52.50 is allocated to unit B.

2. Allocate equity based on institution's actual ratio of capital to assets. Continuing with this example, the institution has capital of $200 and assets of $2,900. Its actual capital-to-assets ratio is 6.9 percent ($200 ÷ $2,900 = 6.9%). Thus, the equity is allocated to the lending units at 6.9 percent of their assets as shown in the following:

	Unit A	Unit B
*Loans	$1,000	$700
Actual Capital Percent Requirement	× 6.9%	× 6.9%
	$ 69	$48.30

Thus, $69 is allocated to unit A, and $48.30 is allocated to unit B.

3. Allocate equity based on risk. (This example is a departure from regulatory guidelines on determining capital adequacy using risk-based assets. Instead this example assigns arbitrary risk weights.)

Assume that capital consumption weights (points) are given for various risk levels. A level of one is minimal risk. A level of 10 is maximum. The risk levels used here are examples only and do not reflect the true risk of the associated lending sectors. Also, this list is not comprehensive. It is only presented to give an idea of how this method works:

Issues

Type of Loan	Balance				Points
Domestic Unit A					
Agriculture	$200	×	8	=	1,600
Manufacturing	300	×	8	=	2,400
Energy	400	×	7	=	2,800
Transportation	100	×	9	=	900
Total	$1,000				7,700
International Unit B					
Agriculture:					
Developed Country	200	×	8	=	1,600
Developing Country	100	×	10	=	1,000
Manufacturing:					
Developed Country	100	×	8	=	800
Developing Country	100	×	9	=	900
Energy:					
Developed Country	100	×	8	=	800
Developing Country	100	×	10	=	1,000
Transportation—None					
Total	$ 700				6,100

* Assume they have no other assets.

Unit A has 7,700 points and unit B has 6,100 points. Let us say the weighted average risk adjusted allocation is 7.5 points per $100 in loans. Unit A's points average 7.7 per $100 in loans (7,700 ÷ 100 = 7.7). Therefore, equity is allocated at 7.7 percent (7.7 ÷ 100 = 7.7%) of its loans.

Unit B's points average 8.71 per $100 in loans (6,100 ÷ 700 = 8.71). Therefore, equity is allocated at 8.71 percent of its loans. The allocation is figured this way:

	Unit A	Unit B
Loans	$1,000	$ 700
Allocation Percent	× 7.7%	× 8.71%
	$ 77	$ 61

Therefore, unit A receives a $77 allocation and unit B receives a $61 allocation.

Two basic drawbacks exist in this method. The first is complexity and, hence, the time consumed to administer and understand the process. Second, reconciliation issues may arise concerning the institution's total equity. Under this method, it is possible to overallocate equity.

If your choice is to allocate equity, a practical approach is to do so according to the following considerations and constraints:

1. Allocate to profit centers only.
2. Allocate either to a department or to lowest responsibility center level.
3. Retain residuals in a corporate pool.
4. Provide an implicit earnings credit for allocated equity.
5. Use regulatory guidelines of capital to assets as a basis for assigning equity. If you also decide to allocate to fee only services units, such as cash management services, modify the formula. Have the modification reflect the institution's expectation for return on equity.
6. Use equity allocation as a performance measurement tool based on ROE calculations.

Each of these points will be discussed further as follows:

1. Allocate to profit centers only.

   The interest of allocating equity is to provide a measurement tool for return on equity. If equity were allocated to nonincome producing centers (cost centers) or net fund providers, there would be no way to apply the ROE measurement criteria. Also, there would be an issue of whether to reallocate the equity from cost centers and net fund providers to profit centers.

2. Allocate either to a department or to lowest responsibility center level.

   There are several organization hierarchy levels where equity could be assigned. It should only be assigned at one level throughout the institution. Let's take an institution that has four levels beneath the corporate structure.

>Corporate Level (Total Institution)
>Group Level
>Division Level
>Department Level
>Unit-Lowest Responsibility Center Level

There is no right or wrong level where equity should be assigned. The level that best fits an institution's needs, philosophy, and reporting structure is where it should be.

3. Retain residuals in a corporate pool.

    Depending on what formula is used, there may be residuals. Some institutions allocate residuals as a percent to total of prior equity allocations. The purpose of allocating residuals has to be questioned particularly because doing so modifies previously determined formulas. (See item 6 which covers the formula.)

4. Provide an implicit earnings credit for allocated equity.

    Some institutions do not provide an earnings credit for allocated equity because it would be at cross-purposes with their funds transfer pricing structure. Others see it as a double benefit because it is free funds to the recipient, who also is receiving an earnings (funds providing) credit.

5. Use regulatory guidelines of weighted average capital to assets as a basis for assigning equity. Modify the formula for fee-income-only-generators, based on an expected ROE.

    Many institutions use an approximation of the regulatory requirements ratio of assets to capital as a proxy for allocating equity. The common practice is to allocate equity based on a profit center's loans, fixed assets, and fee services (with modifications), set out as follows:

    Loans—If the regulatory requirement is for example 7.5 percent of capital to assets, an institution could assign capital to a profit center using this ratio. A profit center

that has $1,000m in loans would receive an equity alloca-
tion of $75m ($1,000m × 7.5% = $75m). Assume the pretax
profit for this center $10m for one year. Using an abbrevi-
ated formula, the pretax ROE for this center is 13.3 percent ($10m ÷ $75m = 13.3%).

Fixed Assets—If an operations center has $3.7 million in
fixed assets (computers and other equipment) it would
receive an equity allocation of $277.5m ($3,700m × 7.5% =
$277.5m).

Fee-Service Business—Furniture and equipment are the
only assets a fee-service business generally has. There are
some fee-service-only organizations in an institution. An
example is cash-management services. The formula for
assigning equity to a non-asset-based profit center has to
be different.

Equity can be allocated several ways to this kind of business.
Obviously, any approach is arbitrary. Let's take one approach and
see how it works. Assume the reason for assigning equity is to get
some kind of measurement on return on equity. Suppose the institution has a stated ROE objective of 18 percent. One approach is to
set a profit goal but not assign equity. For example, say an institution has its cash management services, e.g., remittance processing-
lock box, domiciled in one profit center. Its revenue is $1.5mm per
year and the expenses are $1.3mm per year leaving a pretax profit
of $200m. Senior management has set a goal of $270m. Instead of
assigning equity to this service, assume the institution sets a return
on revenue (ROR) goal of 18 percent. The profit goal is determined
by simply multiplying either the expected or historical revenue by
18 percent. Here $1,500 is multiplied by 18 percent. The profit goal
is $270m. Under this method, you aren't really allocating equity.
Instead you are simulating the process with a more appropriate
ROR measurement.

If one were to assign equity based on the previous 18 percent
standard, then $1,500m would have to be assigned. This could be
arrived at by dividing an expected pretax profit of $270m by 18
percent. Hence $270m ÷ 0.18% = $1,500m. This amount of equity
could be inordinately high, however. It would be the same amount

of equity required to support $20,000m in assets. ($1,500m ÷ 7.5% = $20,000m.) Whatever the base, whether it be revenue or profit, the return standard would drive either an expected profit or equity allocation.

Keep in mind that when equity is assigned to fee-based services, a potential overallocation of corporate equity arises.

6. Use equity allocation as a performance measurement tool based on ROE calculations.

   This provides another performance measurement tool. It augments the common measurements of profitability and return on assets (ROA).

Summary

The allocation issues covered in this chapter are important in providing organizational performance information to management. It is vital to determine an institution's intended use of the information and its management's philosophy.

10

Recovery and Reporting Issues

In preparing reports there are several philosophical issues to be resolved. The most frequently discussed issues include reporting income tax expense, recovering charge-back variances, recovering overhead, notational reporting, foreign exchange expense variance reporting, and prior period adjustments.

Each of these issues is discussed in this chapter. The issue is explained and alternatives are presented. Institutions differ on selection of alternatives to use. Selection is a function of management philosophy. For example, one institution may have a bottom line profitability reporting philosophy for all profit centers. Therefore, they may charge each profit center its fair share of income tax expense. Another institution may only hold a profit center accountable for contribution margin profitability. These would exclude income tax expense charges on their profit center reports. This and the other issues mentioned are covered in this chapter. The intent of this chapter is to equip those who prepare reports and those who receive them with an understanding of the impact of each issue on performance reporting. Clarity on these issues will help an institution's management to decide how to select their position on each one.

Reporting Tax Expense

Two general issues must be resolved in reporting income taxes in management accounting reports. They are (1) whether to report profit center income on a before- or after-tax basis and (2) what rate to use.

On the first issue, the possibilities include reporting profit center income (1) before taxes, (2) after taxes, or (3) before and after taxes. The decision may be based on the desire to only hold the tax department accountable for tax performance issues and not burden profit center reports with an additional line item. If the profit center reports reflect income on an after-tax basis, the philosophy here would be to report each profit center as if it were a separate entity. Hence, the need to state a profit center's after-tax income. Some institutions report income both before and after tax, allowing flexibility on how to interpret profit-center performance.

On the second issue the possibilities include (1) use of a statutory rate or (2) use of the effective tax rate. Also, a side issue is whether to use the same rate for all entities.

The statutory rate is theoretical and does not always reflect business reality but may be appropriate for some business entities. If the statutory rate is applied to all entities in the institution, there is a potential for overrecovery of taxes. This is especially true for larger institutions that have subsidiaries with various businesses. Therefore, it may be prudent to use multiple statutory rates where a variety of businesses exist. The variations could include ordinary income; capital gains; federal, state, and city taxes; possible credit for foreign taxes; leasing business; and nontaxable income.

Using an effective rate brings entity reporting closer to business reality. If used, the decision must be made on whether to apply a general corporate rate or a rate that recognizes the business of each entity.

The more one applies individual considerations, such as individual rates, the more time used in administering the process. Using the effective tax rate is especially apropos when an institution has tax-loss carry forwards.

You must keep in mind the degree of taxation and tax planning usually uncontrollable is at the profit center level. If income taxes are reported, it may be best to segregate them from controllable expenses. The reporting of income on an after-tax basis may influence profit centers to begin, continue, expand, or cancel certain kinds of business transactions.

A companion issue is whether to gross up nontaxable profit-center income and post it on the same basis as though it was taxable. This allows the presentation of tax-exempt income on an equivalent basis with taxable income.

During periods when the institution may not have a tax liability, such as a loss carry forward, it is not appropriate to tax gross-up revenue. This would tend to motivate managers to generate tax-exempt businesses when they aren't beneficial to the institution as a whole.

Recovering Charge-Back Variances

When an institution charges its internal users for operations and data processing services, a recovery issue has to be resolved (see Figure 46). What should be done with over and under recoveries? Some institutions handle this issue by creating management pools in service centers. These pools are pseudo-responsibility centers. All variations would go into a responsibility center, where accountability is matched with responsibility. An institution could have one pool or several, depending on how it wants to track variances.

Another way to handle over and under recoveries is to allocate them to the users based on their percentage of the total charges for services used. Under this method, a service center would have a zero net expense after the over and under recoveries were allocated.

Some institutions handle residual service-center expenses by making them part of their overhead allocation. This tends to spread the residuals burden over the entire institution. Too, it avoids the origin and accountability of these expenses.

Recovering Overhead

Profit center reports can have either a line for overhead items or not be assessed, depending on management philosophy. An institution that views each profit center as a separate and distinct entity

Figure 46
DP Center Recovery Example

An example of a DP Center that places its residuals in a management pool is as follows:

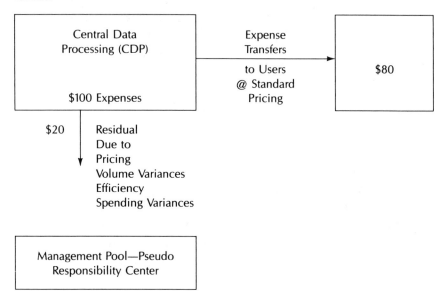

may assign overhead to it. Thus, a profit center absorbs its share of expenses. Some call this the "fully absorbed" approach.

There are various overhead levels: local overhead, service-center overhead, staff overhead, and institutional overhead. The list could go on.

Local overhead represents direct and indirect expenses that organizationally are close to the receiving responsibility center. Local overhead could represent administration expenses for management above a particular department or group. Service center overhead represents the costs of internal services provided to responsibility centers from service centers. Those are expenses that have not been transferred. An example is central data processing (CDP). It is a service center. Some institutions do not transfer expenses directly, instead they construct an overhead rate and allocate CDP expenses. This would be classified as service center overhead throughout the institution. Staff overhead consists of expenses incurred by staff departments, such as human resources, controller's, and economics.

An institution defines its overhead levels by the design of its cost and profitability reporting system. There is no right number of levels. However, the fewer the line items a profit center has to contend with the better. Overhead allocations can be classified as direct support, indirect support, and institutional.

Direct support may be viewed as those items a profit center can manage and control. Hence, they are listed as controllable. Indirect support may be viewed as a remote support function and, therefore, fall into the noncontrollable category. Institutional overhead would be considered a noncontrollable item that exists for the benefit of the entire institution.

Service center variances can be sorted into three categories: volume variances, spending variances, and efficiency variances. In tracking variances by these categories, management can decide more clearly what to do with them. For example, it can adjust rates to accommodate volume fluctuations and, thereby, reduce variations in this category. Also, areas needing attention can be spotted when spending and efficiency variances are known.

In a profit center's report, expenses should be posted in two broad categories, direct and indirect.

Notational Reporting (Shadow Accounting)

Notational reporting is a process in management accounting that accommodates reporting that differs from legal entity financial accounting. This reporting of information is a memo because it does not add up to a reconcilable total. Sometimes it is called shadow accounting. Typical notational reporting includes: double counting, splitting, loan garaging, and memo reporting. Each of these will be explained later.

Notational reporting is used to report management information in a dimension that is in lieu of formal financial and management accounting. It is derived from an alternative perspective. This occurs when management wishes to recognize factors affecting performance different from that in formal management reporting accounts and format. An example is double counting revenue, which occurs when two organizations each receive credit for the same revenue. For example, total revenue is $100. Organization A receives credit for $100, and organization B also receives credit for $100.

Since this inflates reported revenue, it is usually done on a notational (memo) basis. In other words, there is no intent to tie to or reconcile with the books of the institution. The memo is in addition to what is formally stated in the management and financial accounting reports.

Notational reporting exists to recognize factors outside the normal reporting structure. It is a motivational tool. Sometimes an organization is instrumental in generating new business but does not receive credit for it in the normal reporting structure. Notational reporting facilitates this recognition.

The four types of notational reporting are explained below:

Double Counting

Double counting occurs when two or more responsibility centers receive full credit for the same thing. It results in doubling the reported numbers. Double-counted items may include revenue and balances. Double counting is usually done as a means of motivating behavior in a particular direction. It also may be used in performance assessment to recognize the efforts of personnel outside the normal reporting structure. However, double counting has a tendency to distort performance and weaken management control.

Splitting

Splitting occurs when two or more responsibility centers are to share a proration of credit or charges for the same thing. The aggregate results equal 100 percent of the original item. Split or shared items may include revenue, expense, and balances. Splitting can either be within formal management accounting reporting or a notational item. It depends largely on management philosophy.

Loan Garaging

Loan garaging is a common practice and occurs when a loan is booked in an office (branch) that is separate from the originating office (branch) of the loan officer. An example: An Asian territory originated loan, which is booked at the Frankfurt branch for convenience of the account officer, customer, or for tax purposes. The loan may be for the Asian subsidiary of a German firm.

For collection and administration of the loan, the account officer decides it should reside in Germany where the parent company is based. The normal revenue, expense, and balance reporting for the loan would be in Frankfurt where it was booked. In the financial accounting reports, the Frankfurt branch would receive the revenue expense and balance recognition for the loan. However,the formal reporting would not recognize the revenue, expense, and loan balance for the Asian territory. Therefore, a notational report could be developed that reports the revenue, expense, and balance on an Asian territorial basis.

As with this example, a notational report that aligns garaged loans with originating territories is done to report territorial profitability and balances. It separates location profitability from territorial profitability.

Memo Reporting

Below-the-line memos are usually reported when the management accountant wants to highlight a change, exception, or alternative. Sometimes this is done by labeling a line item as "memo" or making an asterisk notation with a corresponding footnote. An example of change is "prior period changes." The management accountant could show the amount of change in a line or column labeled "prior period changes." He or she would not have it affect current month totals but include it in year-to-date figures.

Notational reports can confuse managers because they represent a second set of numbers. They should be labeled as notational and clearly differentiated as a variation from the formal management accounts.

To maintain numerical integrity, notational reporting should be a subset of formal financial and management accounting reports. Unfortunately, not all institutions are clear on this view. Some institutions do not make a distinction of notational reporting. To correct this and prevent confusion, notational reports should be kept separate and labeled as notational. In most situations, notational data should not be an additive in formal management accounting information. That is, it should be nonadditive subset reporting.

In using notational reporting, consider the following factors:

- Intended use and impact of notational reporting.
- Use as a performance reporting mechanism.
- Reconciliation problems.
- Motivation issues.
- Organizational goals.
- Management philosophy.

Here are questions to ask on each point:

1. What is the intended use and impact of notational reporting? Why is notational reporting being used? Is it being used to offset structural deficiencies in reporting? Are there special deals crossing departmental lines that started notational reporting? Is it the best way to report the information? Are other alternatives and resources required?

2. How is it used as a performance reporting mechanism? Will it distort or enhance performance measurement?

3. Are there any reconciliation problems?

Will it reconcile to financial and management accounting? Are the differences clear enough to be understood? Is the procedure well documented?

4. What are the motivation issues?
   Will it motivate staff in the right direction?

5. What are the organizational goals?
   Does the notational reporting produce information that is compatible with organization goals?

6. What is management's philosophy?
   Is the notational reporting compatible with management philosophy? For example, if management concurs with splitting rather than double counting, does the notational reporting reflect that preference?

There are three formality levels of reporting financial information (see Figure 47). The most formal type of reporting is financial accounting. It represents the centrality of financial data for an institution and serves as a basis for formal management accounting. Management accounting is usually unofficial but formal. Its process is arbitrary and depends on good judgment. There is a great deal of breadth on how to determine management accounting methodology. In this regard notational reporting is viewed as a subset of management accounting.

Here's an example of an institution where two organizational units are generating revenue from the same customer. Unit A may

Figure 47
Formality Levels of Accounting

Financial Accounting	Management Accounting	Notational Reporting
Official accounts used for external reporting such as regulatory agencies, stockholders, and the public at large. Uses general ledger data.	Usually unofficial but formal management accounting is used for internal management reporting.	Unofficial and nonformal use of management accounting. Used for internal management reporting as a means to accommodate unusual situations.

have developed business by getting a new client and setting up a lending relationship. Unit B may be involved by garaging (booking) the loan and servicing it. Both units may want credit for their work. The possibilities include:

1. Giving unit A all the revenue credit.
2. Giving unit B all the revenue credit.
3. Redefining the organizations.
4. Giving units A and B each full revenue credit by double counting.
5. Splitting the revenue between units A and B.

Obviously, the two units would have to agree on using options 1 and 2. If both of them are classified as profit centers, it may be difficult in getting them to agree on a 100 percent and 0 percent arrangement.

With option 3, some institutions have redefined organizations from profit centers to cost centers in dealing with this issue. This can be more acceptable if the newly defined cost center can be viewed as a stand-alone product. For example, a loan syndications unit is a profit center, and management would like to lump the revenue generated by it with that of other units. The decision is to treat loan syndications as a support function. Certainly, its manager would like to get credit for the generated income. By defining loan syndications as a cost center, the issue of who gets credit revenue is resolved. However, this may not be to the satisfaction of the loan syndications manager.

The organization's revenue is booked into the lending units. Therefore, lending units receive 100 percent of the revenue and loan syndications receive 0 percent.

You could classify the product revenue as "loan syndication fees." Under this scenario, the loan syndications manager receives two reports. One report is for his or her cost center and does not report revenue. The cost center only reports administrative expenses. The other report is for his or her product called "loan syndications" and data related revenue and expense. The profitability dimensions are then clearly delineated. They would appear as follows:

	Unit A	Unit B	Product: "Loan Syndications"
Organization Profitability	Revenue	Expense Only (Cost Center)	
Product Profitability			Revenue and Expense

Under this arrangement there is no double counting. Instead, measurements of accountability are clearly defined.

If option 4 (double counting) were used, then the participating units each would receive full revenue credit. For example, if units A and B participated in either the acquisition or maintenance of a loan and the revenue was say $100 credit, the institution's reporting would appear as follows:

General Ledger		Shadow Accounting	
Loan Revenue	$100	Unit A—Loan Revenue	$100
		Unit B—Loan Revenue	$100
Total	$100	Total	$200

Obviously, more income has been reported in shadow accounting than exists.

This option has appeal because each unit is motivated to participate in acquiring and maintaining loans. Organization profitability results are distorted, however, by double counting. It detracts from clarity in reporting performance. Hence, some management control is lost in following a policy of double counting.

Some institutions overcome this objection by following option 5, which is splitting revenue. For example, splitting revenue between units A and B is an option. The revenue split would be agreed to by all parties and management. This option tends to motivate both units to continue a joint business arrangement. It also preserves the integrity of reported information. Revenue between units A and B could be split on a 60–40 percent basis. If there was $100 in revenue, unit A would receive $60 and unit B, $40. The numbers could easily reconcile with the general ledger as follows:

General Ledger		Shadow Accounting	
Loan Revenue	$100	Unit A—Loan Revenue	$ 60
		Unit B—Loan Revenue	$ 40
Total	$100	Total	$100

Here's a recap on how these options compare:

	Revenue		
		Shadow Accounting	
	General Ledger	Unit A	Unit B
Option 1 Give Unit A All the Revenue Credit	$100	$100	0
Option 2 Give Unit B All the Revenue Credit	$100	0	$100
Option 3 Redefine Units between Profit Centers and Cost Centers; Products	$100	Distribution varies with definition	
Option 4 Give Units A and B Revenue Credit (Double Count)	$100	$100	$100
Option 5 Split the Revenue between Units A and B	$100	$ 60	$ 40

Foreign Exchange Expense Variance Reporting

Some institutions have foreign units and use dual currency reporting. For budget control, special analyses must determine the impact of spending variances caused by foreign exchange fluctuations. Budgeting for a foreign unit is usually prepared in that country's currency and there normally is a head office translation rate. For example, the American head office staff would translate the budget into U.S. currency at a stated rate.

A financial institution has a London branch that budgets 60,000 British pounds sterling for stationery and supplies. The planned translation rate is 1.45 U.S. dollars to the British pound.

The financial institution's U.S. headquarters would look at the expenditure as $87,000 (60,000 × 1.45 = $87,000).

At the end of the year, only $80,000 was spent. This results in a favorable variance of $7,000. But say the translation rate was $1.20 U.S. to the British pound (average translation rate for the year). This provides more information on the variance. It can now be explained as follows:

$80,000	Actually Spent ÷ by $1.20, the Actual Translation Rate = 66,667 British Pounds Spent
66,667	Pounds Spent
− 60,000	Pounds Budgeted
6,667	Unfavorable Spending Variance in Pounds

6,667 pounds unfavorable spending variance × $1.20 actual translation rate = $8,000 unfavorable spending variance (in U.S. dollars).

If we take the earlier variance of $7,000 and add the unfavorable spending variance of $8,000 to it, this results in a favorable translation variance of $15,000 ($7,000 + $8,000 = $15,000).

Here's how to recap the variance calculation:

$15,000	Favorable Translation Variance ($1.45 − $1.20 = $0.25) ($0.25 × 60,000 = $15,000)
−$ 8,000	Unfavorable Spending Variance (6,667 × $1.20 = $8,000 Rounded)
$ 7,000	Net Favorable Variance

By doing these analyses you can sort out the controllable spending variances from the uncontrollable translation rates. Management, thus, has the ability to assess performance more clearly.

Prior Period Adjustments

When changes are made in the current month that affect previous months, a decision must be made on how to report it. The options are:

1. Adjust the month it occurred (history) and hence year-to-date. Do not highlight or flag the changes in the current month.

2. Report prior period adjustments in the current month. Do not change history. Adjustments are reflected in year-to-date.

3. Report prior period adjustments as a separate item in the current month. Reflect change in year-to-date numbers. Adjust the month it occurred in next month's report and drop the prior period adjustments notation.

Option 1 is to adjust history and year-to-date but not show any change in the current month.

Under this option, the reader of a report would have difficulty noticing any prior period adjustments. The significance of changes or corrections gets buried. The changes should be clearly discernible. One advantage of this option is that current reported data is not distorted by listing prior period adjustments in the current month. Here is how this option would work:

Report with No Adjustments

	Jan.	Feb.	Mar.	Apr.	Current Month May	Year-to-Date
Expenses	20	25	21	15	10	91

Report with Additional Expenses of $6 That Occurred in March

	Jan.	Feb.	Mar.	Apr.	Current Month May	Year-to-Date
Expenses	20	25	27	15	10	97

As you can see, a prior period adjustment was done in May for March. Only the historical data (March) was adjusted. This also affects the year-to-date total.

Option 2 takes the position of only reporting prior period adjustments in the current month. History would not be changed. However, the adjustment would be reflected in the year-to-date total. The report would appear as follows:

Report with No Adjustments

	Jan.	Feb.	Mar.	Apr.	Current Month May	Year-to-Date
Expenses	20	25	21	15	10	91

Report With Additional Expenses of $6 That Occurred in March.

	Jan.	Feb.	Mar.	Apr.	Current Month May	Year-to-Date
Expenses	20	25	21	15	16	97

The disadvantage of this method is the impact it has on current month reported results. It, therefore, can distort the current month's reported results.

Option 3 under this method is reporting prior period adjustments as a separate item in the report. The adjustment is reflected in the year-to-date numbers. The current month numbers are not affected. The following month's report would drop the item as prior period adjustment and put it into the month it occurred. Using the same example, assume an adjustment for the month of March is being made in the current month's report (May), as follows:

Report with No Adjustments

	Jan.	Feb.	Mar.	Apr.	Current Month May	Year-to-Date
Expenses	20	25	21	15	10	91

Report with Adjustments

	Jan.	Feb.	Mar.	Apr.	Current Month May	Prior Period Adjustment	Year-to-Date
Expenses	20	25	21	15	10	6	97

Assume next month's (June) report reflected usual expenses of $12, as follows:

	Jan.	Feb.	Mar.	Apr.	May	Current Month June	Prior Period Adjustment	Year-to-Date
Expenses	20	25	27	15	10	12	0	109

The $6 adjustment was taken out of the prior period adjustments column and placed in the March column.

This option has considerable merit. It does not affect current period reporting and highlights a prior period change. Finally, it places that adjustment with the month it applies to.

Summary

No particularly right or wrong method exists for each of the management accounting issues discussed in this chapter. This is because management accounting is mostly for internal management use and measures performance based on the institution's philosophy. The right method will motivate behavior according to the insitution's wishes and will measure performance according to its philosophy (see Figure 48).

Some methods make more sense than others. Also, some are more popular. The choice of method can be made based on what is best for the institution given its culture and philosophy.

Most of the issues discussed have several variations. Only the basic alternatives were discussed here. Each alternative has numerous variations.

Figure 48
Management Accounting Issues

Issue	Summary of Issue	Possible Solutions	Cross-Impact of Possible Solutions			
			Allocation of Cost of Carry for Nonearning Assets	Allocation of Capital (Equity)	Profit Center Profitability	Behavioral Impact and Issues of Possible Solutions
Prior Period Adjustments	The issue is whether or not to impact current period reporting with prior period adjustments.	1. Impact current period data with prior period adjustments. 2. Impact prior period only with adjustments. Report as memo only in current period.			1—Will increase or decrease profitability depending on nature of adjustment. 2—No impact on current period. Will impact prior periods and hence year-to-date.	1—Reporting current period data with prior period adjustments distorts current performance. It could confuse management and influence misguided decisions. 2—Placing adjustments in prior period and only memo reporting in current period places undistorted results for the period.
Funds Transfer Pricing (FTP)	The issue is how to construct an FTP that is perceived as being equitable, motivates staff in a desired direction, and is cost-effective to administer.	1. Use single-pool rate for charge and credit for funds. 2. Use multiple-pool rates for charge and credit for funds. 3. Use matched funding for charge and credit for funds.	1, 2, & 3—Rate structure will affect cost of carry charged to responsibility centers.	1, 2, & 3—Will impact methodology for providing funding credit or assessing charges for capital.	1, 2, & 3—Rate structure will impact profitability	1, 2, & 3—Depending on rate structure, profit center managers could either be motivated or demotivated toward providing funds and lending. Rate structure for charge and credit for funds significantly influences deposit acquisition and lending activity.

Figure 48 (Continued)

Issue	Summary of Issue	Possible Solutions	Cross-Impact of Possible Solutions		Behavioral Impact and Issues of Possible Solutions
			Recovery of Overhead	Profit Center Profitability	
Reporting Profit Center Profitability after Taxes	The issue is whether to report profit center profitability on an after-tax basis.	1. Report profitability after taxes. 2. Report profitability before taxes. 3. Report profitability both before and after taxes.	1 & 3—Depending on definition of what is included in overhead, reporting of taxes may reduce amount of overhead to be recovered.	1 & 3—Profitability is reduced when reported after tax unless there is a benefit for losses. 2—Profitability is shielded from tax assessments/benefits when reported on a before-tax basis. Tax gross-ups and tax-equivalent income adjustments will change profitability.	1—Some profit center managers view taxes as a corporate accountability beyond their control. Hence, taxes are viewed by some as a nonessential line item. 2—Reporting profit center profitability before taxes will cause managers to focus on controllable performance. However, it may cause an overly optimistic assessment of profitability. 3—Reporting profits on a before- and after-tax basis provides a balanced view.

Figure 48 (Continued)

			Cross-Impact of Possible Solutions				
Issue	Summary of Issue	Possible Solutions	Allocation of Loan Losses	Allocation of Loan Loss Reserves	Prior Period Adjustments	Profit Center Profitability	Behavioral Impact and Issues of Possible Solutions
Allocation of Loan Losses	The issue is whether or not to charge profit centers for loan write-offs.	1. Assign actual losses to originating lending units. 2. Spread losses to all lending units. 3. Do not allocate losses; retain in corporate pool.		1 & 2—If reserves are allocated the reserve levels would have to be adjusted. 3—If the reserves are allocated they would have to be reconciled or adjusted to corporate balances. If reserves are not allocated there is no impact.	1 & 2—Depending on timing, losses may cause prior period adjustments.	1 & 2—Assignment of loan losses affects profit center profitability.	1—Assigning loan losses may cause a conscious behavior toward loan quality. 2—Spreading loan losses may demotivate those units who have high-quality loans. 3—By not allocating losses quality emphasis may be difficult to communicate.
Allocation of Loan Loss Reserves	The issue is whether or not to allocate loan loss reserves to profit centers.	1. Allocate reserves based on specific risk rating factors. 2. Allocate reserves based on an overall factor, for example, 1% of outstanding balances. 3. Do not allocate reserves.	1&2—If losses are assigned then reserves may have to be adjusted as loans are written off. 1 & 2—If losses are not assigned then reserves will only fluctuate due to normal balance changes.			1 & 2—Initial allocation of reserves to profit centers may not affect profitability. However, provisions taken out to increase reserves will decrease profitability. Saleback of reserves from profit centers could result in increased profitability.	1—Allocating reserves with specific factors provides insight on loan quality and raises awareness levels of areas requiring management attention. 2—Allocating reserves with an overall factor may demotivate those units who have high-quality loans and provide distorted and masked reporting where significant low-quality loans exist. 3—If reserves are not allocated, quality awareness may deteriorate.

Figure 48 (Continued)

Cross-Impact of Possible Solutions

	Possible Solutions	Allocation of Capital (Equity)	Recovery of Overhead	Funds Transfer Pricing (FTP)	Profit Center Profitability	Behavioral Impact and Issues of Possible Solutions
Allocation of Cost of Carry for Nonearning Assets	The issue is whether or not to charge responsibility centers for nonearning assets such as fixed assets and nonperforming loans.	1—Allocation of funding cost for nonearning assets may influence method for allocating capital.	1—Allocation of funding cost for nonearning assets reduces unassigned overhead.	1—Allocation of funding cost may influence FTP methodology.	1—Allocation of funding cost will decrease profitability.	1—Allocation of funding cost for nonearning assets will raise awareness and motivate conservation of funds uses. 2—By not allocating cost of carry, users could be inclined toward suboptimal use of funds.
	1. Allocate funding cost for nonearning assets to responsibility centers. 2. Do not allocate funding costs.					

	Possible Solutions	Allocation of Cost of Carry for Nonearning Assets		Funds Transfer Pricing	Profit Center Profitability	Behavioral Impact and Issues of Possible Solutions
Allocation of Capital (Equity)	The issues are: whether or not to allocate equity; what types of responsibility centers to receive allocations; and whether to give credit or charge for allocated capital.	1, 2, & 3—Allocating capital influences determination of funding sources for nonearning assets.		1, 2, & 3—Allocating capital influences FTP methodology.	1, 2, & 3—Depending on how capital allocation influences FTP methodology, it may increase or decrease profitability.	1, 2, & 3—Allocation of capital raises awareness of finite resources available to the institution. Will cause decisions that are more capital-conscious. Charges and credits will motivate behavior according to perception on how fair is the method being used.
	1. Allocate capital with no charge or credit for capital provided. 2. Allocate with charge for capital provided. 3. Allocate capital and give credit for capital provided. 4. Don't allocate capital.					

Figure 48 (Continued)

| | | | | Cross-Impact of Possible Solutions | | |
Issue	Summary of Issue	Possible Solutions	Charge-Back of Expense Transfer Variations	Recovery of Overhead	Profit Center Profitability	Behavioral Impact and Issues of Possible Solutions
Charge-Back of Expense Transfer Variations	The issue is whether or not to charge responsibility centers for service center variances.	1. Retain variances in service center pool. 2. Transfer out variances based on user volume.		1—Retaining variances may increase overhead pool. 2—Transferring out variances may reduce overhead pool.	1—Retaining variances may increase profitability. 2—Transferring out variances may reduce profitability.	1—Retaining variances in management pool will motivate service center management toward more efficient and cost-effective operations. 2—Transferring out variances to users will tend to weaken their budget control and predictability of costs.
Recovery of Overhead	The issue is whether or not to charge responsibility centers for overhead. Also, to what degree should products and centers be burdened?	1. Allocate all overhead expense to responsibility centers and products. 2. Allocate all overhead to profit centers and products only. 3. Retain overhead in a corporate unassigned pool.	1 & 3—If transfer variances are held in service center pools, then allocating overhead will tend to spread these variances to a wider base. If variances are charged back, then there will be no impact.		1 & 2—Allocating overhead will tend to decrease profitability. If initially allocated to all responsibility centers, then it will have to be reallocated to profit centers.	1 & 2—Allocating overhead to profit centers creates a full absorption mindset that holds centers responsible for covering the institution's overhead. 3—Retaining overhead in an unassigned pool may cause personnel to overlook its cost. It could motivate decisions in a direction other than intended.

Figure 48 (Continued)

Issue	Summary of Issue	Possible Solutions				Cross-Impact of Possible Solutions	Behavioral Impact and Issues of Possible Solutions
						Profit Center Profitability	
Shadow Accounting	The issue is whether to double count or split revenues among responsibility centers for shared businesses.	1. Double count revenue among profit centers. 2. Split revenue between profit centers. 3. Don't double count or split revenue.				1—Double counting will increase profitability. It will also report higher-than-actual earnings. 2—Revenue splitting will impact individual profit centers but not the total of all.	1—Since double counting distorts profitability, it could confuse management and thereby contribute to poor decisions. It also weakens budget control. 2—Revenue splitting requires negotiations but does not inflate reported revenue as does double counting. Creates a realistic perspective. 3—By not recognizing participants, it may demotivate them from generating business that will benefit others.
						Profit Center Profitability	
Foreign Exchange Variance Analysis	The issue is whether to report the impact of foreign exchange translation variances on a regular basis. Plan-to-actual comparisons of revenue and experience.	1. Regular reporting and variance analysis. 2. Infrequent analysis of variances.				No impact.	1 & 2—Analyzing variances provides management with decision tools relative to volume variances, spending variances, and foreign exchange variances. Provides a perspectivce on budget-to-actual. Strengthens management control.

Appendix

Key Performance Ratios

Earnings

- **Net Interest Margin (NIM) (%)**
  Formula:

$$\frac{\text{Interest Income} - \text{Interest Expense}}{\text{Average Total Earning Assets}} = \text{NIM}$$

This shows the percentage point difference between the yield and the cost of funds for interest-bearing instruments. The difference at least should be positive.

- Return on Average Assets (ROA) (%)
  Formula:

$$\frac{\text{Current Net Income/(Loss), Annualized}}{\text{Average Assets, Annualized}} = \text{ROA}$$

This is a common measurement that shows the performance of the institution's assets. A normal performance is positive.

- **Return on Equity (ROE) (%)**
  Formula: (one method)

$$\frac{\text{Current Net Income/(Loss), Annualized}}{\text{Average Total GAAP}^* \text{ Net Worth}} = \text{ROE}$$

---

* Generally Accepted Accounting Principles.

This ratio reflects the return on equity performance of the institution. A positive ROE is normal.

- **Earnings per Share (EPS) ($)**

    Formula:

    $$\frac{\text{Net Income Available to Common Stockholders}}{\text{Number of Shares of Common Stock Outstanding}} = \text{EPS}$$

    EPS measures the return of income on a per share basis. The normal balance is positive.

Credit Risk

- **Delinquent Loan Balances to Total Loans (%)**

    Formula:

    $$\frac{\text{Delinquent Loan Balances}}{\text{Total Loans}} = \text{Ratio}$$

    This ratio indicates the percentage of the loan portfolio that is delinquent.

- **Loan Loss Reserves to Total Loans (%)**

    Formula:

    $$\frac{\text{Loan Loss Reserves}}{\text{Total Loans}} = \text{Ratio}$$

    This ratio shows the adequacy of loss reserves to total loans. The ratio should reflect an assessment of the known percentage of bad loans to total loans.

- **Charge-offs ($)**

    Formula:

    Amount of Loans Charged Off This Month/Quarter

    When compared against delinquent loan balances this measures how much of the bad loans are being recognized as noncollectible.

Funding

- **Core Deposits to Financial Liabilities**

  Formula:

  $$\frac{\text{Transaction} + \text{Savings}}{\text{Financial Liabilities}} = \text{Ratio}$$

  This ratio reflects the level of core deposits to the financial liabilities. A higher ratio indicates a more stable funding portfolio.

- **Withdrawal Ratio**

  Formula:

  $$\frac{\text{Beginning Core Deposits (Transaction} + \text{Savings)}}{\text{Ending Core Deposits (Transaction} + \text{Savings)}} = \text{Ratio}$$

  The withdrawal ratio is a measure of how successful the institution is retaining core deposits. A ratio of less than 100 percent is good.

Liquidity

- **Asset Liquidity (%)**

  Formula:

  $$\frac{\text{Cash plus Unpledged Investment Securities}}{\text{Total Assets}} = \text{Asset Liquidity}$$

  This measure shows the ratio of liquid funds to assets. The higher the ratio, the more able the institution is to respond to decreases in deposits.

- **Liability Liquidity (%)**

  Formula:

  $$\frac{\text{Total Borrowings}}{\text{Total Deposits}} = \text{Liability Liquidity}$$

This measure shows how volatile the institution's funding is to borrowings. Borrowings are not as stable as core deposits. A lower ratio is good.

$$\frac{\text{Cash} + \text{Free Investments}}{\text{Total Liabilities (exclude deferred taxes, mortgage)}}$$

Capital Adequacy

- **Regulatory Net Worth**

  Formula:

  $$\frac{\text{Net Worth}}{\text{Assets}} = \%$$

  (or for S&Ls)

  $$\frac{\text{Net Worth}}{\text{Liabilities}} = \%$$

  This is a measurement of financial health of an institution. A higher ratio is good.

- **GAAP Net Worth (%)**

  $$\frac{\text{GAAP Net Worth}}{\text{Assets}} = \%$$

  GAAP net worth requirements tend to be more severe than regulatory requirements. Hence the ratio may be lower than regulatory net worth to assets. A higher ratio is good.

- **Loans to Capital**

  Formula:

  $$\frac{\text{Loans}}{\text{Regulatory Net Worth}} = \%$$

  This is a measure of how much loans are leveraged to net worth. A lower ratio is good.

Asset and Liability Management

- **Interest-Rate Sensitivity [Rate-Sensitive Assets (RSAs) to Rate-Sensitive Liabilities (RSLs)]**

Formula:

$$\frac{\text{Interest Sensitive Assets}}{\text{Interest Sensitive Liabilities}} = \%$$

This is one measure of an institution's exposure to interest-rate risk. A ratio of 1.0 is generally good. This means there is a match between RSAs and RSLs.

- **Funding Maturity Gap**

  Assets to Liabilities ≤ 1 Year (%)

  Formula:

  $$\frac{\text{Assets} \leq 1 \text{ Year}}{\text{Liabilities} \leq 1 \text{ Year}} = \%$$

  This measure determines if a gap will exist within the next 12 months on funding the assets.

  Assets to Liabilities 1 Year (%)

  $$\frac{\text{Formula} > 1 \text{ Year}}{\text{Liabilities} > 1 \text{ Year}} = \%$$

  This is a measure to determine if a gap will appear beyond the next year on funding the assets.

- **Earning Assets to Total Assets**

  Formula:

  $$\frac{\text{Earning Assets}}{\text{Total Assets}} = \%$$

  This is a measure to determine the earning posture of the institution's assets. A higher ratio is good.

Operating

- **Full-Time Equivalent Staff**

  Formula:

  $$\frac{\text{Average Paid Hours per Staff} \times \text{Number of Staff}}{\text{Average Work Hours in the Month per Staff} \times \text{Number of Staff}} = \begin{array}{l}\text{Number} \\ \text{and/or} \\ \text{Decimal} \\ \text{Fraction}\end{array}$$

This is a measure of the staff equivalency. It is more reliable than regular staff count.

Graphs

Net Interest Margin (NIM)

$$\frac{\text{Interest Income} - \text{Interest Expense}}{\text{Average Total Earning Assets}} = \text{NIM}$$

Return on Average Assets (ROA)

$$\frac{\text{Current Net Income/(Loss), Annualized}}{\text{Average Assets, Annualized}} = \text{ROA}$$

Return on Average Equity (ROE)

[one method]

$$\text{Current Net Income/(Loss), Annualized} = \text{ROE}$$

Earnings Drag of Delinquent Loans

[two methods]
(1) Accrued Interest Income Reversed Due to Delinquencies
(2) Cost of Funding of Delinquencies over 30* Days

Asset Liquidity

$$\frac{\text{Cash and Investment Securities}}{\text{Total Assets}} = \text{Asset Liquidity}$$

Cash and demand deposits plus U.S. Government and agency securities plus common and preferred stock, except regulatory agency capital, plus other investments plus accrued interest receivable minus valuation allowances.

Liability Liquidity

$$\frac{\text{Total Borrowings}}{\text{Total Deposits}} = \text{Liability Liquidity}$$

---

*Or another specification.

Regulatory agency advances plus [other borrowed money: commercial bank loans plus reverse repurchase plus consumer retail repurchase agreements plus overdrafts in demand deposits plus commercial paper issued] plus subordinated debentures not qualifying for net worth plus mortgage-backed bonds issued plus other borrowings.

Yields

Defined as:

Interest Income as a Percentage of Average Assets

$$\frac{\text{Interest on Loans} + \text{Investment Securities} + \text{Deposits} + \text{Income from Financing Leases}}{\text{Average Total Assets}} = \text{Yield}$$

Cost of Funds

Net Interest on Deposits plus Interest on Borrowed Money = Cost of Funds

Regulatory Net Worth

Preferred Stock plus Guaranty Stock plus Paid-in Surplus plus Capital Certificates plus Subordinated Debentures plus Appraised Equity Capital plus Net Worth Certificates plus Reserves plus Undivided Profits (retained earnings) plus Net Undistributed Income.

Check current regulations on this definition.

Generally Accepted Accounting Principles (GAAP) Net Worth

Retained Earnings plus Common Stock plus Preferred Stock plus Additional Paid-in Capital plus Income Capital Certificates (certain issues) less Foreign Currency Adjustments less Marketable Equity Security Adjustments.

Check current specifications on this definition.

Appendix

Interest-Rate Sensitivity

Rate-Sensitive Assets less Rate-Sensitive Liabilities=Interest Rate-Sensitivity Position

$$\frac{\text{Rate–Sensitive Assets}}{\text{Rate–Sensitive Liabilities}} = \text{Interest Rate Sensitivity Ratio}$$

Spread Management

Average Yields – Average Cost of Funds = Average Spread

(Transaction plus Savings) Withdrawal Ratio

$$\frac{\text{Beginning Balances}}{\text{Ending Balances}} = \text{Savings Withdrawal Ratio}$$

Less than 100% = Good

Glossary

ALCO (Asset and Liability Committee). A committee of key staff that sets policy and makes decisions regarding asset and liability management.

ALM (Asset and Liability Management). The process of managing the net earnings impact of balance sheet risk including interest rate risk, liquidity risk, and capital adequacy risk.

Average Item Cost. The cost of an object as determined by direct and indirect expense identification techniques using the formula total costs divided by total volume equals average item cost per unit.

Business Entity. A responsibility center (RC) or group of RCs involved in a similar business enterprise as an organization.

Capital Budget. A schedule of planned capital expenditures.

Charge-Back Variance. A variance resulting in either an over-recovery or under-recovery for services charged to users.

CIF (Customer Information File). A file of information on customer relationships, segments, and demographics.

COF (Cost of Funds). The cost, expressed either in percentage points or amount, of funds.

Contract Spread. A basis point spread for funding a loan usually agreed to by the treasury (money desk) and the lending officer.

Cost. The attribution of direct and indirect expenses toward an object such as a product or service.

Cost of Capital. The cost attributable to obtaining capital (funds).

Credit Risk. The risk of a customer not repaying his or her loan.

Customer Profitability. The profitability of a customer relationship. This usually applies to large corporate customer relationships.

DDA. Demand Deposit Account.

Duration. A quantitative technique used in asset and liability management to analyze the cash flow implications of a balance sheet occurrence.

Equity. Assets minus Liabilities.

Equity Allocation. A management accounting procedure that allocates equity to responsibility centers (usually income producing) to establish a basis for performance measurement.

Financial Accounting. Accounting by general ledger and reporting on the financial condition of an institution.

Float. Uncollected funds.

Foreign Exchange Risk. The risk of a net position in a currency that is deteriorating.

FTE (Full-Time Equivalent Staff). Staff equivalency expressed in decimal fractions based on hours.

Funding. The process of providing funds for assets.

Funds Transfer Pricing. Placing a value on funds provided and funds used to provide a credit and charge, respectively.

Gap Management. A technique that analyzes the gap between rate-sensitive assets and rate-sensitive liabilities.

Interest-Rate Risk. The risk in which interest rate movements affect net interest income.

KPI (Key Performance Indicator). An indicator based on a key output.

Leverage. The ratio of assets or loans to equity and/or deposits.

Liquidity. The ability to fund assets and meet the withdrawal demands of depositors.

Loan Garaging. The process of booking a loan in a branch that may or may not be in the same territory of origination.

Loan Loss Allocation. A process that allocates loan losses to business entities based on a specified formula or criteria.

Management Accounting. A function that uses financial accounting and other data and rearranges it into information for management decision making.

Matched Funding. Occurs when interest rates on funding assets are matched with maturity and risk.

MIRS (Management Information Reporting System). A system that reports information to management.

Multiple-Pool Method. A funds transfer pricing method that uses more than one interest-rate source.

Notational Reporting. Sometimes referred to as shadow accounting. The process of reporting information in an informal organization matrix.

Operating Risk [Snafu risk]. The risk that something may be done in error or may not get done at all.

Optimization. A technique of developing the best scenario in asset/liability mix and hence the best possible net interest income.

Overhead Recovery. A process of charging out overhead to selected responsibility centers. The amount of these charges recovered.

Preplan—Preliminary Plan. A step in the planning cycle that usually involves summary level data. Occurs in midyear.

Prior Period Adjustments. Adjustments made that recognize changes to data generated in prior periods.

Product. The lowest level of service that attracts revenue.

Productivity. Output as compared to input.

Profitability Triad. Organizational, product, and customer profitability.

ROA (Return on Assets). The ratio of net earnings to assets.

ROE (Return on Equity). The ratio of net earnings to equity.

RSA (Rate-Sensitive Assets). Assets subject to interest rate changes and, hence, repricing.

RSL (Rate-Sensitive Liabilities). Liabilities subject to interest rate changes and, hence, repricing.

Responsibility Center. A defined entity where formal expense tracking occurs.

Sector Risk. Risk associated with a specified sector such as a geographic sector.

Sensitivity Analysis. What-if analysis. Uses a number of gaming scenarios.

Shadow Reporting. Same as notational reporting. A form of matrix reporting.

Simulation. Uses sensitivity analyses to find alternative solutions given different variables.

Single-Pool Method. A basic form of funds transfer pricing that uses one rate for providers and users.

Standard Cost. A prescriptive cost. It is what the cost should be given a certain volume, work measurement, and spending level.

Strategic Plan. Long-range plan. Usually three to five years in the future.

Strategic Planning. The process of conducting forward long-range planning.

SWOT (Strengths, Weaknesses, Opportunities, Threats). Self-analysis criteria used in strategic planning.

Tactical Plan. A short-range plan. Usually one year or less. Commonly called the operating plan.

Tactical Planning. The process of performing a short-term plan.

Transfer Risk. The risk of funds being blocked when transferring currency from one currency to another.

Bibliography

Books

Allen, Paul H., *Reengineering the Bank*, Chicago: Probus Publishing Co., 1994.

Arnott, Robert D. and Frank J. Fabozzi, *Active Asset Allocation*, Chicago: Probus Publishing Co., 1992.

Austin, Douglas V. and and Paul Simoff, *Strategic Planning for Banks*, Chicago: Probus Publishing Co, 1991.

Bank Administration Manual, 3rd Edition, Chicago: Probus Publishing Co., 1988.

Banks, Erik, *Complex Derivatives*, Chicago: Probus Publishing Co., 1994.

Belasco, Kent S., *Bank Productivity: Improvement Techniques*, Chicago: Probus Publishing Co., 1990.

Bird, Anat, *SuperCommunity Banking*, Chicago: Probus Publishing Co., 1993.

Bollenbacher, George M., *The New Business of Banking*, Chicago: Probus Publishing Co., 1992.

Brown, Albert J., *The High Performance Bank*, Chicago: Probus Publishing Co., 1991.

Chorafas, Dimitris N., *Chaos Theory in the Financial Markets*, Chicago: Probus Publishing Co., 1994

Cole, Leonard P., *Cost Accounting for Financial Institutions*, Chicago: Probus Publishing Co., 1994.

Cox, Edwin B. et al., *Bank Director's Handbook, 2nd Edition*, Auburn House, 1986.

Dattatreya, Ravi E. et al., *Interest Rate and Currency Swaps*, Chicago: Probus Publishing Co., 1994.

255

Bibliography

Ernst and Young, *Performance Measurement for Financial Institutions*, Chicago: Probus Publishing Co., 1994.

Fabozzi, Frank J. and Atsuo Konishi, *Asset/Liability Management*, Chicago: Probus Publishing Co., 1994.

Freedman, Roy A. et al., *Artificial Intelligence in the Capital Markets*, Chicago: Probus Publishing Co., 1994.

Gup, Benton E. and Robert Brooks, *Interest Rate Risk Management*, Chicago: Probus Publishing Co., 1993.

Hempel, George H. and Donald G. Simonson, *Bank Financial Management*, New York: Wiley, 1991.

Johnson, Hazel J., *Bank Asset/Liability Management*, Chicago: Probus Publishing Co., 1994.

Mackinzie, Jeff L. and Keith Schap, *Financial Engineering with Basis Trading*, Chicago: Probus Publishing Co., 1994.

Markovich, Denise, *Effective Asset/Liability Management for the Community Bank*, Chicago: Probus Publishing Co., 1990.

Mayland, Paul F., *Bank Operating Credit Risk*, Chicago: Probus Publishing Co., 1993.

McCoy, John B. et al., *Bottomline Banking*, Chicago: Probus Publishing Co., 1993.

Thornbill, William T., *Effective Risk Management for Financial Organizations*, 1989.

Trippi, Robert R. and Efraim Turban, *Neural Networks in Finance and Investing*, Chicago: Probus Publishing Co., 1993.

Trippi, Robert R. and Jae K. Lee, *State-of-the Art Portfolio Selection*, Chicago: Probus Publishing Co., 1992.

Uyemura, Dennis G. and Donald van Deventer, *Financial Risk Management in Banking*, Chicago: Probus Publishing Co., 1993.

Wold, Geoffrey H., and Robert F. Shriver, *Strategic Systems Planning for Financial Institutions*, Chicago: Probus Publishing Co., 1993.

Wyderko, Leonard, *A Practical Guide to Duration Analysis*, Chicago: Probus Publishing Co., 1989.

Periodicals

Anonymous, "An Analyst's View of Bank Profitability," *Bankers Magazine*, May/Jun 1990, pp 5–10.

Anonymous, "The Bank Management Formula," *Bank Management*, May 1993, p 36

Anonymous, "Be Customer-Focused, Learn from Retailers," *Bank Management*, Jan/Feb 1994, pp 14–15.

Anonymous, "The Challenge in Merging Product Lines," *Bank Management*, Oct 1993, p 16.

Anonymous, "Portfolio Management Strategies," *Bank Management*, Jan/Feb 1994, pp 56–60.

Anonymous, "Top 100 Performance Rating," *Bank Management*, May 1993, pp 43–44.

Arnold, William M. Jr., "Risk Management's New Look," *Bankers Magazine*, Sep-Oct 1991, pp 60–66.

Baker, William L., "Looking for Success in All the Right Places?" *Texas Banking*, Sep 1993, p 27.

Barry, John F., "Strategic Planning Top CFO Priority," *Bank Management*, Jan/Feb 1994, p 12–14.

Berger, Allen N. and David B. Humphrey, "The Dominance of Inefficiencies over Scale and Product Mix Economies in Banking," *Journal of Monetary Economics*, Aug 1991, pp 117–148.

Boyle, Alexander R.M., "The Future of American Banking—Managing for Change," *Bankers Magazine*, Sep/Oct 1993, pp 77–79.

Brennan, Peter J., "Profitability Software: To Be Competitive, Instinct, Intuition No Longer Enough," *Bank Management*, Jan 1992, pp 51–54.

Cantrell, Wanda and Mary Colby, "Getting a Grip on Information," *Bank Management*, Sep 1993, pp 22–28.

Cantrell, Wanda and Mark Borowsky, "Reinventing the Bank," *Bank Management*, Aug 1993, pp 26–32.

Carey, Tom, "Business Strategies for Financial Services," *Banking World*, Sep 1993, pp 60–61.

Clark, James, "Cost of Capital versus ROE: A Major Challenge for Thrifts," *Bankers Magazine*, May/Jun 1992, pp 50–54.

Cuddy, Robert W., "Evaluating Bank Management," *Bottomline*, Sep/Oct 1991, pp 41, 50.

Bibliography

Davis, Steven, "The Role of Leadership," *Banking World*, May 1992, pp 22–24.

Giokas, D. and M. Vassiloglou, "A Goal Programming Model for Bank Assets and Liabilities Management," *European Journal of Operational Research*, Jan 7, 1991, pp 48–60.

Grunewald, Alan E., "Financial Models Work Well at Heart of A/L Programs," *Bank Management*, Oct 1990, pp 74–77.

Haisten, Marilyn, "TQM Really Begins with 'M'," *Credit Union Management*, Jan 1994, pp 23–25.

Hewitt, Janet Reilley, "Management Uncertainty," *Mortgage Banking*, Apr 1993, p 4.

Johannes, James M., "Beyond Textbook Asset-Liability Management," *Journal of Retail Banking*, Fall 1992, pp 23–27.

Kearney, Kevin J., "Forces for Change in Banking," *World of Banking*, Jan/Feb 1992, pp 18–21.

Langen, Dieter, "An (Interactive) Decision Support System for Bank Asset Liability Management," *Decision Support Systems*, Dec 1989, pp 389–401.

Maruko, Maya, "Banks Need Streamlining, Management Restructuring," *Japan Times Weekly International Edition*, Sep 28–Oct 4, 1992, p 19.

McCuistion, Niki, "The Trek toward TQM," *Credit Union Mangement*, Jan 1994, pp 21, 25.

McGee, William M. and Michael J. May, "Realizing a Management Information System's Potential," *Bankers Magazine*, Sep/Oct 1993, pp 15–20.

Motley, L. Biff, "Re-engineering Should Help Marketers," *Bank Marketing*, Jan 1994, p 60.

Paradise-Tornow, Carol A., "Management Effectiveness, Service Quality, and Organizational Performance in Banks," *Human Resource Planning*, 1991, pp 129–139.

Payant, W. Randall, "Understanding Interest Rate Risk," *Bank Management*, Jun 1992, pp 70–73.

Rauch, Karl, "Developing a Relationship-Based Sales Culture," *Bankers Magazine*, Sep/Oct 1993, pp 49–54.

Richardson, Gerald M., "Downsizing Should Be Part of a Comprehensive Plan," *Bank Management*, Nov 1991, pp 49–51.

Rosenberg, Richard M., "Success Components for the 21st Century," *Bank Management*, Jan/Feb 1994, pp 32–39.

Seital, Fraser P., "20-20 Leadership," *United States Banker*, Sep 1993, p 70.

Sellers, Bob L., "How to Become a High Performance Bank," *Texas Banking*, Aug 1991, p 32.

Shawkey, Bruce, "Star Performers: Six Credit Union CEOs Tell Why 'Getting By' Isn't Enough," *Credit Union Magazine*, Nov 1992, pp 64–73.

Shay, Rodger, "Liability Management Strategies," *Savings and Community Banker*, Feb 1994, pp 40–41.

Siems, Thomas F., "Quantifying Management's Role in Bank Survival," *Economic Review*, First Quarter 1992, pp 29–41.

Smith, Brian P, "Interest Rate Risk Alternatives Demand Careful Analysis," *Savings Institutions*, Nov 1991, pp 48–49.

Swift, Clinton R., "Data for Decision Makers," *Bank Management*, Apr 1991, pp 40–44.

Taylor, Jeremy F., "A New Approach to Asset/Liability Management," *Bankers Magazine*, Mar/Apr 1993, pp 32–39.

Taylor, David Van L., "Banks Develop Risk Assessment Methodology," *Bank Management*, Feb 1991, pp 48–50.

Thompson, Carolyn, "Operating the TQM Way," *Credit Union Management*, Jan 1994, pp 34–36.

Violano, Michael, "The Team Approach to Bank Technology Management," *Bankers Monthly*, Nov 1992, pp 22–23.

Weiss, Stuart, "Swaps, Caps, Swaptions, Captions, and Other Interest Rate Hedges," *CFO: The Magazine for Chief Financial Officers*, Feb 1990, pp 49–52.

Wyatt, Craig, "Outlook for Banking: Adapting to Change," *Bank Management*, Sep 1993, pp 12–15.

Index

technology research and, 26
writing a strategic plan, 31-33
Swarm theory, 138
SWOT
  questions, 21-22
  using, to review an organization,
    27-29

T

Tactical Planning
  see also Planning
  in asset and liability management,
    118-119
  capital expenditures budgeting, 53,
    56

balance sheet planning, 41-46
budgeting process and, 37-57
definition of, 19
expense planning, 47-53
main areas of, include, 37
managements' review of
    preliminary plan in, 39-40
planning retreat, 40
plan reviews, 41
preliminary plan in, 39
presentation to the board, 41
regular (financial/operating) plan,
    40-41
revenue planning, 46-47
steps in, 39-41, 58

About the Author

Leonard P. Cole, a consultant to financial institutions, lives near San Diego, California. He specializes in performance measurement, executive information and control reporting, profit improvement, cost and profitability reporting, and management accounting issues.

Mr. Cole was senior manager with Price Waterhouse. While in that position he was the management accounting national product manager for their financial services product group. He directed cost accounting, profitability measurement, and management information reporting projects.

Before becoming a consultant, Mr. Cole was a vice-president of a large West Coast bank where he managed several financial administration functions including cost analysis, financial analysis, and international planning and reporting. He also served as a senior staff member in asset and liability management.

A frequent speaker, Mr. Cole has spoken at several conferences, including the Council on International Banking (CIB), Bank Administration Institute (BAI), the National Commercial Finance Association (NCFA), and the National Association for Bank Cost and Management Accounting (aka NABCA).

He is a faculty member at the University of Southern California, California State University, San Marcos, and the University of Phoenix. He holds B.S. and M.B.A. degrees from the University of Southern California. He is also the author of *Cost Accounting for Financial Institutions*.